Daily Prayer

GUIDE TO THE SEASONS

Give praise to the Father almighty,
to his Son, Jesus Christ, the Lord,
to the Spirit who dwells in our hearts,
both now and for ever. Amen.

The Lord's Prayer

Traditional version:

Our Father, who art in heaven,
hallowed be thy name,
thy kingdom come, thy will be done,
on earth as it is in heaven.
Give us this day our daily bread,
and forgive us our trespasses,
as we forgive those who trespass against us.
And lead us not into temptation,
but deliver us from evil.
For thine is the kingdom, the power and the glory,
for ever and ever. Amen.

Modern version:

Our Father in heaven,
hallowed be your name,
your kingdom come,
your will be done,
on earth as in heaven.
Give us today our daily bread.
Forgive us our sins
as we forgive those who sin against us.
Save us from the time of trial
and deliver us from evil.
For the kingdom, the power, and the glory are yours
now and for ever. Amen.

Daily Prayer

A form of praise and prayer
for use at any time of the day

Compiled by

BRUCE CARLIN and TOM JAMIESON

DARTON·LONGMAN + TODD

First published in 2002 by
Darton, Longman and Todd Ltd
1 Spencer Court
140–142 Wandsworth High Street
London SW18 4JJ

Compilation © 2002 Bruce Carlin and Tom Jamieson

The right of Bruce Carlin and Tom Jamieson to be identified as the Compilers of this work has been
asserted in accordance with the Copyright, Designs and Patents Act 1988.

ISBN 0–232–52445–9

A catalogue record for this book is available from the British Library.

Designed and produced by Sandie Boccacci
using QuarkXPress on an Apple Power Mac 7500
Illustrated by Leigh Hurlock
Printed and bound in Great Britain by
The Cromwell Press, Trowbridge, Wiltshire

CONTENTS

FOREWORD

Many lay people, as well as clergy, look for help with a pattern of daily prayer. Very often it is a question of how to get started, and this highlights the need for an accessible form of 'office'.

I believe that *Daily Prayer* provides this in a form which varies with the seasons and is adaptable to personal circumstances. My own use of *Daily Prayer* encourages me to think that it provides a doorway into prayer, in a simple and yet disciplined way, which leads into ever greater depth. There is no doubt that our increasing awareness of God comes through a regular discipline. *Daily Prayer* provides the framework for that.

Although *Daily Prayer* is now used widely within the churches, it has its origin in experimental use in the Diocese of Durham and we are grateful to Bruce Carlin and Tom Jamieson for their diligent research and imaginative presentation.

MICHAEL DUNELM:

Auckland Castle, Bishop Auckland,
County Durham

PREFACE

Welcome to *Daily Prayer*. We trust that you will find it a useful resource on your spiritual journey.

Before being published, *Daily Prayer* has been used in experimental forms by people from all walks of life, laity and clergy, and corporately by some church communities. Their feedback has enabled us to develop it into this final form.

We have aimed to make *Daily Prayer* easy to use for the beginner while still fulfilling the needs of those more experienced in prayer. It can be used on its own or supplemented with other material. A brief introduction follows on page 1, and detailed notes on how to use it are in the Commentary, beginning on page 169.

Daily Prayer is commended to, and has been used by, lay and ordained Christians of all denominations. For Anglican clergy we would like to suggest that *Daily Prayer* fulfils the canonical obligation to say the daily office if *Prayer in the Morning* or *Evening* is also used. *Daily Prayer* also provides the basis for *A Service of the Word* as envisaged in Common Worship, though if used as the principal Sunday service it should have a penitential rite and an affirmation of faith added.

The version of the psalms printed in *Daily Prayer* is that of The Grail Translation (New Inclusive Language Version), and for consistency of style we recommend that you use this for the psalms set in the Lectionary. This Psalter is published inexpensively in paperback by HarperCollins (ISBN 0 00 627939 2).

Should you wish to contact us for further advice on using *Daily Prayer* you can obtain our postal addresses from Crockford's Clerical Directory (available at most main libraries), or see our web site at:

> http://www.communigate.co.uk/ne/dailyprayer

or contact us by e-mail at:

> Daily.Prayer@durham.anglican.org

TOM JAMIESON and BRUCE CARLIN

INTRODUCTION

Recent years have seen a rediscovery of the value of a structured form for our daily prayers. Several recent publications are in response to this recovery of the 'Daily Office' tradition of praying. This book is exceptional among them in offering a once-a-day main prayer time, in contrast to the traditional morning and evening twofold pattern: 'a bold decision which makes a lot of sense,' as one commentator put it.

The heart of this book is seven different orders for *Daily Prayer* to use in slow rotation through the seasons of the Christian Year, with another for use on Saints' and Holy Days. The Contents page sets out this scheme and the Lectionary pages keep you right as to the time to move from one order to another. Each of these orders has the same clear structure, while the texts vary through the seasons, and through the days of the week in each season. The aim is to provide the right balance of simplicity, continuity and variety in the 'diet' of daily prayer. Structure and balance are explored further in the Commentary, beginning on page 169.

Full use of these orders requires a Psalter (the Book of Psalms in a translation suited to recitation) and a Bible, as well as this book. On occasion (such as while travelling) when a Psalter and Bible are not available, the Psalms and Readings for During the Day from the section *Prayer Through the Day* (from page 115) can be used instead.

In addition to the orders for *Daily Prayer* there are short, simple and self-contained orders for *Prayer in the Morning* and *Prayer in the Evening*. These may be used instead of, or as well as, *Daily Prayer* to provide up to a threefold pattern of daily prayer.

A *Vigil of the Resurrection* is also provided for use on Saturday evening as the beginning of the observance of Sunday. Such a pattern has ancient origins, especially in the Orthodox churches, and also echoes the eve of Sabbath ceremonies of the Jewish people.

HOW TO USE *DAILY PRAYER*

When?

Set aside 20 minutes or longer each day, at whatever time of day suits your schedule. Crack of dawn, coffee time, lunch break, before tea, or last thing. This is your *Daily Prayer* time. On those days when you just won't have 20 minutes of peace, you can turn to the shorter forms from page 115. *Prayer in the Morning* or *Evening* can be said in, well, the time it takes to boil a kettle if you must! Some people will use these shorter forms as well as *Daily Prayer* to provide three times of prayer each day.

Where?

A place set aside is best, whether at home, in church, or the workplace. For some it may be on the train. The shorter forms are especially suited to use while travelling as you do not need any other book with them.

With whom?

Though you may usually pray alone, this form of ordered prayer draws you into the corporate prayer of the whole Church. That is why praying 'we' and 'us' makes sense, even when you are alone. If you can, even occasionally, be part of a small group which says *Daily Prayer* together, that will be a bonus.

What do I need?

As well as this book, a Bible, and ideally a Psalter (you could use the psalms from your Bible but a psalter is a better translation for prayer). You might wish to use additional resources such as a hymn-book, a Collect, a prayer diary, a book of spiritual readings, a candle, icon, flowers, etc.

Knowing your way round **Daily Prayer**

Each order has the same very simple format. The Opening page is followed by the page for the day of the week; and then the final three pages conclude the order. *Saints' and Holy Days*, and *The Seasons of Passion* and *Resurrection* are just a little different.

The Contents page gives a handy guide to which order you should use, and the Lectionary also guides you from season to season. A loose card contains the Doxology ('Give praise to the Father ...') that should follow the psalms and most of the canticles, together with two versions of the Lord's Prayer. You will soon know these by heart.

Daily Prayer will flow more smoothly if you spend a moment marking up the psalm and reading from the Lectionary before you begin.

The Lectionary

The following pages contain the scheme for the recitation of the psalms and reading of Scripture in *Daily Prayer*. A detailed explanation of this can be found in the Commentary (page 169) which we recommend that you read, but a few brief notes follow.

The psalm references given are those of The Grail Translation (New Inclusive Language Version), which is the version used in the psalm portions that are printed in this book. If you are using the Grail Psalter ignore the psalm number in parentheses. If you are using a different version of the Psalter you may find that on occasions where a whole psalm is not set you may have to use your judgement as to which verses are intended.

The Bible references are those of the New Revised Standard Version, and the same problem may occasionally arise if you use a different translation of Scripture. A detailed explanation of how to read the Bible references can be found in the Commentary (page 172).

In the seasons there is only one set of readings which repeats each year, while in *Through the Year* there is a three-year cycle, following that of the Revised Common Lectionary which is used in many churches. A key to which calendar year corresponds to Years A,B,C can be found at the beginning of *Through the Year* (page 81).

The Lectionary follows the calendar date except during Lent and Eastertide, which move from year to year. At the beginning of Lent simply break off the calendar readings and go to those for *The Season of Penitence*, resuming the dated readings on the Monday after Pentecost.

From time to time the Lectionary is interrupted by the celebration of a Saint or Holy Day. The Psalm and Reading is given for the festival and a category of the festival is given in parentheses. These categories are used in the order for *Saints' and Holy Days* (page 93) in the same way as are the days of the week in other parts of *Daily Prayer*.

JANUARY – THE SEASON OF THE WORD MADE FLESH (Page 31)

Date	Psalm	Scripture	Season of the Word Made Flesh
1	Naming of Jesus – use Sunday texts – Psalm 103 – Acts 3:1–4:12			
2	2, 8	Heb. 8:1–7; 9:11–28	
3	19	Hebrews 10:5–25	The Season of the Word Made Flesh
4	23, 29	Heb. 12:1–4,18–29	
5	33	Heb. 13:1–19	
6	Epiphany – use Wednesday texts – Psalm 113 – Jeremiah 31:7–14, 31–34			
7	4, 16	Genesis 12:1–9	
8	17	Gen. 18:1–15; 21:1–8	
9	18:2–30	Gen. 22:1–19	
10	18:31–51	Gen. 28:10–22	
11	40	Exodus 3:1–17	
12	45	Judges 6:11–24,36–40	
13	46, 101	Judg. 13	
14	57	1 Samuel 3	
15	61, 99	1 Kings 3:4–15	The Season of the Word Made Flesh
16	63	1 Ki. 19	
17	67, 138	Heb. 1	
18	125, 133, 134	Ephesians 1:1–14	
19	72	Eph. 1:15–2:10	
20	76	Eph. 2:11–22	
21	84, 127	Eph. 3:1–13	
22	89:2–19	Eph. 3:14–21	
23	89:20–53	Eph. 4:1–16	
24	122, 126	Eph. 4:17–5:2	
25	Conversion of St Paul – Saints (AE) – Psalm 66 – Philippians 3:1–14			
26	91	Eph. 5:3–20	
27	96	Eph. 5:21–6:9	
28	97	Eph. 6:10–24	The Season of the Word Made Flesh
29	131, 150	John 1:1–18	
30	146	John 1:19–34	
31	147	John 1:35–51	
FEBRUARY			
1	148	John 2:1–12	The Season of the Word Made Flesh
2	Presentation – use Friday texts – Psalm 48 – Romans 11:33–12:5			

FEBRUARY – THROUGH THE YEAR (Page 81)

Date	Psalm	Year A	Year B	Year C
		Use the psalms and readings from this table only until Shrove Tuesday,		
		then go to The Season of Penitence (Lectionary page 6).		
3	104:1–24	Genesis 1:1–2:4a	Genesis 37	Exodus 15:19–16:8
4	104:24–35	Gen. 2:4b–25	Gen. 39	Exod. 16:9–35
5	119:1–24	Gen. 3	Gen. 40:1–41:13	Exod. 17:8–18:12
6	1, 3, 4	Gen. 4:1–16	Gen. 41:14–57	Exod. 18:13–27
7	10	Gen. 6:5–7:24	Gen. 42	Exod. 19
8	19	Gen. 8:1–9:17	Gen. 43	Deuteronomy 5:6–21
9	23, 30	Gen. 11:1–9	Gen. 44	Exod. 24
10	32, 36	Gen. 11:27–12:9	Gen. 45	Exod. 32
11	34	Gen. 13	Gen. 46:1–7,28–47:6	Exod. 33
12	37:1–20	Gen. 14	Gen. 47:13–31	Exod. 34:1–9,28–35
13	37:21–40	Gen. 15	Gen. 49	Exod. 35:20–36:7
14	42, 43	Gen. 16:1–17:16	Gen. 50:1–6,12–26	Exod. 37:1–9; 39:32–43
15	45	Gen. 18:1–15	Exodus 1:1–2:10	Numbers 9:15–23
16	46	Gen. 18:16–33	Exod. 2:11–25	Num. 13:1–2,16–14:9
17	119:25–48	Gen. 19:1–29	Exod. 3	Num. 20:1–13
18	57	Gen. 21:1–21	Exod. 4:1–23	Num. 20:22–29; 21:4–9
19	60	Gen. 22:1–19	Exod. 5:1–6:13	Deut. 5:1–5a; 6:1–9
20	61, 62	Gen. 23	Exod. 6:28–7:13	Deut. 8
21	63	Gen. 24:1–49	Psalm 105:1–6,26–38	Leviticus 25:1–24
22	65, 150	Gen. 24:50–67	Exod. 12:1–14,28–42	Deut. 14:22–15:11
23	67, 82	Gen. 25:7–11,19–34	1 Corinthians 1:1–17	Deut. 16:1–17
24	77	Gen. 27:1–45	1 Cor. 1:18–31	Deut. 27:11–28:14
25	80	Gen. 28:10–29:14a	1 Cor. 2	Deut. 30:15–20; 34
26	81	Gen. 31:1–21	1 Cor. 3	Joshua 1
27	84	Gen. 32:3–32	1 Cor. 4	Josh. 2:1–3:1,14–17
28	90	Gen. 33; 35:9–29	1 Cor. 5	Josh. 4:19–24; 6
29	95	Jude	Jude	Jude

MARCH – THROUGH THE YEAR (Page 81)

Date	Psalm	Year A	Year B	Year C
		Use the psalms and readings from this table only until Shrove Tuesday,		
		then go to The Season of Penitence (at the foot of this page).		
1	119:49–72	Romans 1:1–15	1 Cor. 6	Josh. 24:1–28
2	91	Rom. 1:16–2:11	1 Cor. 8	2 Corinthians 1:1–22
3	92	Rom. 2:12–3:8	1 Cor. 9:1–14	2 Cor. 1:23–3:3
4	93, 121, 122	Rom. 3:9–31	1 Cor. 9:15–10:13	2 Cor. 3:4–18
5	94	Rom. 4	1 Cor. 10:14–11:1	2 Cor. 4:1–15
6	12, 16	Rom. 5	1 Cor. 11:17–34	2 Cor. 4:16–5:10
7	99, 128	Rom. 6	1 Cor. 12:1–11	2 Cor. 5:11–6:10
8	103	Rom. 7:1–13	1 Cor. 12:12–30	2 Cor. 6:11–7:1
9	114, 146	Rom. 7:14–25	1 Cor. 12:31–13:13	2 Cor. 7:2–16

SAINTS' DAYS IN MARCH AND APRIL

The following Saints' Days occur during March and April
and the order for Saints' Days should be used.
Saints' Days should not be kept on Sundays in Lent or Eastertide, or at all during
Holy Week or Easter Week. They should be transferred to the nearest free day.
We recommend that Scripture readings omitted because of a Saint's Day
should be added to that of the following day.

MARCH

19	*St Joseph – Saints (O) – Psalm 25 – Hebrews 11:1–16*
20	*St Cuthbert – Saints (P) – Psalm 97 – Matthew 9:35–38*
25	*Annunciation of our Lord – Holy Days (L) – Psalms 111, 113 – 1 Chronicles 17:1–14*

APRIL

23	*St George – Saints (M) – Psalm 5 – Hebrews 11:17–12:2*
25	*St Mark – Saints (AE) – Psalm 149 – Mark 16:1–8*

THE SEASON OF PENITENCE (Page 43)

From Ash Wednesday until Pentecost the Lectionary cannot follow the calendar date as Easter
moves. The season of Lent begins with Ash Wednesday and continues as follows.

Wed.	78:1–39	Jeremiah 2:1–13	*Ash Wednesday*
Thur.	78:40–72	John 2:13–25	
Fri.	22	John 3:1–21	*Season of Penitence*
Sat.	119:57–80	John 3:22–36	

Day	Psalm	Scripture	SEASON OF PENITENCE (Page 43)
Sun.	42, 43	Jeremiah 31:27–37	
Mon.	1, 44	John 4:1–42	
Tues.	6, 49	John 4:43–5:18	
Wed.	12, 13, 14	John 5:19–47	1st week of Lent
Thur.	15, 51	John 6:1–21	
Fri.	38	John 6:22–40	
Sat.	119:81–104	John 6:41–71	
Sun.	50	Jeremiah 7:1–15	
Mon.	26, 27	John 7:1–13	
Tues.	28, 32	John 7:14–30	
Wed.	34, 39	John 7:31–52	2nd week of Lent
Thur.	73	John 8:2–11	
Fri.	54, 56	John 8:12–30	
Sat.	119:105–128	John 8:31–59	
Sun.	80	Jeremiah 8:18–9:11	
Mon.	74, 101	John 9	
Tues.	77, 112	John 10:1–21	
Wed.	85, 86	John 10:22–42	3rd week of Lent
Thur.	90, 120	John 11:1–44	
Fri.	70, 140	John 11:45–57	
Sat.	119:129–152	John 12:1–11	
Sun.	147	Jeremiah 18:1–17	
Mon.	103, 123	John 12:12–19	
Tues.	130, 131, 137	John 12:20–36	
Wed.	139	John 12:37–50	4th week of Lent
Thur.	141, 143	John 13:1–20	
Fri.	71	John 13:21–30	
Sat.	119:153–176	John 13:31–38	
Sun.	35	Jeremiah 20:7–18	
Mon.	7	John 14:1–14	
Tues.	17	John 14:15–31	
Wed.	31	John 15:1–17	5th week of Lent
Thur.	41, 64	John 15:18–27	
Fri.	102	John 16:1–15	
Sat.	79, 110	John 16:16–33	

THE SEASON OF THE PASSION – HOLY WEEK (Page 55)

No Saints' Days should be kept this week.

Day	Psalm	Scripture	
Sun.	61, 62	Romans 5:1–11	*Holy Week – Palm Sunday*
Mon.	25	Lamentations 1:1–14	*Holy Week – Monday*
Tues.	55	Lam. 3:1–9, 49–66	*Holy Week – Tuesday*
Wed.	142	Lam. 5	*Holy Week – Wednesday*
Thur.	42, 43	John 17	*Maundy Thursday*
Fri.	69	1 Corinthians 1:18–25	*Good Friday*
Sat.	88	Job 14:1–14	*Holy Saturday*

THE SEASON OF THE RESURRECTION – EASTER WEEK (Page 63)

No Saints' Days should be kept this week.

Sun.	113, 114, 117	2 Corinthians 5:14–6:2	*Easter Day*
Mon.	30	Exodus 5:1–9, 19–6:1	*Easter Monday*
Tues.	29	Exod. 12:21–36	*Easter Tuesday*
Wed.	66	Exod. 12:37–13:2	*Easter Wednesday*
Thur.	81	Exod. 13:17–14:14	*Easter Thursday*
Fri.	135	Exod. 14:15–31	*Easter Friday*
Sat.	118	Exod. 15:1–21	*Easter Saturday*
Sun.	30	Exod. 16:1–3, 13–18, 31–35	*2nd Sunday of Easter*

THE SEASON OF NEW LIFE (Page 69)

Saints' Days should not be kept on Sundays of Easter, but be transferred to Monday.

Mon.	92	John 20:1–18	
Tues.	96	John 20:19–31	
Wed.	97	John 21:1–14	*2nd Week of Eastertide*
Thur.	98	John 21:15–25	
Fri.	105	1 Corinthians 15:1–28	
Sat.	108	1 Cor. 15:35–57	
Sun.	29	1 Peter 1:1–12	
Mon.	115	1 Pet. 1:13–2:10	
Tues.	116	1 Pet. 2:11–25	
Wed.	124, 125	1 Pet. 3:1–12	*3rd Week of Eastertide*
Thur.	129, 138	1 Pet. 3:13–4:6	
Fri.	146	1 Pet. 4:7–19	
Sat.	148	1 Pet. 5	

THE SEASON OF NEW LIFE (Page 69)

SS Philip and James (1 May), St Matthias (14 May), The Visitation (31 May),
and St Barnabas (11 June) may fall during The Season of New Life.
Their Psalms and Readings can be found in the monthly calendars on the following pages.

Day	Psalm	Scripture	Season of New Life
Sun.	66	Revelation 1	
Mon.	9	Rev. 2:1—17	
Tues.	18:2—30	Rev. 2:18—3:6	
Wed.	18:31—51	Rev. 3:7—22	4th Week of Eastertide
Thur.	20, 93	Rev. 4	
Fri.	21	Rev. 5	
Sat.	33	Rev. 7:9—8:1	
Sun.	81	Romans 6:3—11	
Mon.	40	Rev. 11:15—12:17	
Tues.	46, 114	Rev. 14:6—13; 15:1—4	
Wed.	48	Rev. 18:1—3, 9—24	5th Week of Eastertide
Thur.	68	Rev. 20	
Fri.	76	Rev. 21	
Sat.	89:2—19	Rev. 22	
Sun.	135	Romans 12	
Mon.	8, 67	Hebrews 10:1—25	
Tues.	65	Colossians 1:9—27	6th Week of Eastertide
Wed.	72	Philippians 2:1—13	
Thur.	24, 150	Mark 16:9—20	Ascension Day
Fri.	100, 110	Rom. 5:1—11	
Sat.	47, 149	Rom. 8:1—17	6th Week of Eastertide
Sun.	84	Rom. 8:18—39	
Mon.	104:1—24	Numbers 11:16—17, 24—29	
Tues.	104:24—35	1 Samuel 9:27—10:13	
Wed.	107:1—22	1 Sam. 16:1—13	7th Week of Eastertide
Thur.	107:23—43	2 Kings 2:1—15a	
Fri.	111, 126	Ezekiel 37:1—14	
Sat.	145	Joel 2:18—29	
Sun.	147	2 Timothy 1:1—14	Day of Pentecost

Continue with Through the Year, from the calendar date on the following pages.

Date	Psalm	Year A	Year B	Year C
		Some of the Saints in May and June will occur during The Season of New Life.		
		If they fall on a Sunday in that season (or on Trinity Sunday)		
		they should be transferred to Monday.		
I		St Philip and St James — Saints (AE) — Psalm 139 — Proverbs 4:10–18		
		Resume the psalms and readings from this table on the Monday after Pentecost,		
		continuing from whatever the calendar date is.		
		You will find that you resume the Scripture reading from where you left off before Lent.		
11	119:1–24	Genesis 3	Gen. 40:1–41:13	Exodus 17:8–18:12
12	1, 3, 4	Gen. 4:1–16	Gen. 41:14–57	Exod. 18:13–27
13	10	Gen. 6:5–7:24	Gen. 42	Exod. 19
14		St Matthias — Saints (AE) — Psalm 16 — Acts 2:37–47		
15	19	Gen. 8:1–9:17	Gen. 43	Deuteronomy 5:6–21
16	23, 30	Gen. 11:1–9	Gen. 44	Exod. 24
17	32, 36	Gen. 11:27–12:9	Gen. 45	Exod. 32
18	34	Gen. 13	Gen. 46:1–7,28–47:6	Exod. 33
19	37:1–20	Gen. 14	Gen. 47:13–31	Exod. 34:1–9, 28–35
20	37:21–40	Gen. 15	Gen. 49	Exod. 35:20–36:7
21	42, 43	Gen. 16:1–17:16	Gen. 50:1–6, 12–26	Exod. 37:1–9; 39:32–43
22	45	Gen. 18:1–15	Exod. 1:1–2:10	Numbers 9:15–23
23	46	Gen. 18:16–33	Exod. 2:11–25	Num. 13:1–2, 16–14:9
24	119:25–48	Gen. 19:1–29	Exod. 3	Num. 20:1–13
25	57	Gen. 21:1–21	Exod. 4:1–23	Num. 20:22–29; 21:4–9
26	60	Gen. 22:1–19	Exod. 5:1–6:13	Deut. 5:1–5a; 6:1–9
27	61, 62	Gen. 23	Exod. 6:28–7:13	Deut. 8
28	63	Gen. 24:1–49	Psalm 105:1–6, 26–38	Leviticus 25:1–24
29	65, 150	Gen. 24:50–67	Exod. 12:1–14, 28–42	Deut. 14:22–15:11
30	67, 82	Gen. 25:7–11, 19–34	Philemon	Deut. 16:1–17
31		The Visit of Mary to Elizabeth — Saints (VM) — Psalm 85 — Galatians 3:23–4:7		

Date	Psalm	Year A	Year B	Year C
1	77	Gen. 27:1–45	1 Corinthians 1:1–17	Deut. 27:11–28:14
2	80	Gen. 28:10–29:14a	1 Cor. 1:18–31	Deut. 30:15–20; 34
3	81	Gen. 31:1–21	1 Cor. 2	Joshua 1
4	84	Gen. 32:3–32	1 Cor. 3	Josh. 2:1–3:1,14–17
5	90	Gen. 33; 35:9–29	1 Cor. 4	Josh. 4:19–24; 6
6	119:49–72	Romans 1:1–15	1 Cor. 5	Josh. 24:1–28
7	91	Rom. 1:16–2:11	1 Cor. 6	2 Corinthians 1:1–22
8	92	Rom. 2:12–3:8	1 Cor. 8	2 Cor. 1:23–3:3
9	93, 121, 122	Rom. 3:9–31	1 Cor. 9:1–14	2 Cor. 3:4–18
10	94	Rom. 4	1 Cor. 9:15–10:13	2 Cor. 4:1–15
11	St Barnabas – Saints (AE) – Psalm 101 – Acts 4:32–37			
12	12, 16	Rom. 5	1 Cor. 10:14–11:1	2 Cor. 4:16–5:10
13	99, 128	Rom. 6	1 Cor. 11:17–34	2 Cor. 5:11–6:10
14	103	Rom. 7:1–13	1 Cor. 12:1–11	2 Cor. 6:11–7:1
15	107:1–22	Rom. 7:14–25	1 Cor. 12:12–30	2 Cor. 7:2–16
16	107:23–43	Rom. 8:1–17	1 Cor. 12:31–13:13	2 Cor. 8
17	114, 146	Rom. 8:18–39	1 Cor. 14:1–12	2 Cor. 9
18	115	Rom. 9:1–24	1 Cor. 14:13–25	2 Cor. 10
19	119:73–96	Rom. 9:25–10:21	1 Cor. 14:26–40	2 Cor. 11:1–21a
20	116, 117	Rom. 11:1–24	1 Cor. 15:1–11	2 Cor. 11:21b–12:10
21	130, 131, 134	Rom. 11:25–36	1 Cor. 15:12–34	2 Cor. 12:11–13:13
22	136	Rom. 12	1 Cor. 15:35–58	Jonah 1; 2
23	139	Rom. 13	1 Cor. 16	Jonah 3; 4
24	The Birth of John the Baptist – Saints (O) – Psalm 50 – Matthew 11:2–19			
25	85	Rom. 14:1–12	Jeremiah 1:4–10	Esther 2:5–18
26	142, 143	Rom. 14:13–15:6	Luke 4:16–30	Esther 2:19–3:6
27	145	Rom. 15:7–33	Luke 6:12–26	Esther 3:8–4:17
28	147	Rom. 16	Luke 10:1–20	Esther 5
29	St Peter and St Paul – Saints (AE) – Psalm 71 – Galatians 1:11–2:10			
30	148	Prov. 1:20–2:8; 3:1–18	Proverbs 16:16–17:15	Esther 7

The Readings in Year B from 25–28 June

are selected on the theme of vocation, ministry and ordination.

They may be used in any year when this theme is appropriate.

JULY – THROUGH THE YEAR (Page 81)

Date	Psalm	Year A	Year B	Year C
1	1, 4, 15	Proverbs 5:15–6:19	Prov. 22:1–16	Esther 8
2	7	Prov. 8	Prov. 23:19–25; 24:13–22	Esther 9:20–32
3	*St Thomas – Saints (AE) – Psalm 146 – 1 Peter 1:3–9*			
4	119:97–120	Job 1; 2	Prov. 25	Acts 8:25–40
5	8, 12	Job 3	Prov. 27:1–22	Acts 9:1–31
6	9	Job 4:1–9; 5:17–27	Prov. 28:2–16	Acts 9:32–43
7	16, 23	Job 6:1–4; 7:1–21	Prov. 31:10–31	Acts 10
8	17	Job 8:1–7; 9:1–24	1 Timothy 1	Acts 11
9	19	Job 11:1–12; 19:1–29	1 Tim. 2:1–3:13	Acts 12
10	33	Job 20:1–8; 21:1–26	1 Tim. 3:14–4:16	Acts 13:1–12
11	34	Job 22; 23:1, 8–17	1 Tim. 5:1–6:2	Acts 13:13–43
12	38	Job 31	1 Tim. 6:3–21	Acts 13:44–14:7
13	42, 43	Job 38:1–21; 39:26–40:2	2 Timothy 1	Acts 14:8–28
14	46, 96	Job 40:3–14; 42:1–6	2 Tim. 2	Acts 15:1–29
15	48	Job 42:7–17	2 Tim. 3	Acts 15:30–16:5
16	50	Colossians 1:1–14	2 Tim. 4	Acts 16:6–40
17	119:121–144	Col. 1:15–23	James 1	Acts 17:1–15
18	57	Col. 1:24–2:5	Jas. 2	Acts 17:16–34
19	63, 70	Col. 2:6–3:4	Jas. 3	Acts 18:1–23
20	65	Col. 3:5–4:1	Jas. 4	Acts 18:24–19:20
21	67, 97	Col. 4:2–18	Jas. 5	Acts 19:21–20:16
22	*St Mary Magdalene – Saints (O) – Psalms 30, 32 – Luke 7:36–8:3*			
23	73	Song 1:1–2:7	Song 3:6–5:1	Song 6:4–8:4
24	74	Song 2:8–3:5	Song 5:2–6:3	Song 8:5–14
25	*St James – Saints (AE) – Psalms 11, 29 – Luke 9:46–56*			
26	76	Acts 20:16–38	Acts 1	Ezek. 1:1–12, 22–2:10
27	77	Acts 21:1–14	Acts 2:1–36	Ezekiel 3:1–21
28	80	Acts 21:15–36	Acts 2:37–47	Ezek. 10:18–22; 11:14–25
29	81	Acts 21:37–22:29	Acts 3	Ezek. 12:1–16; 13:1–10a
30	84	Acts 22:30–23:11	Acts 4:1–31	Ezek. 18
31	119:153–176	Acts 23:12–35	Acts 4:32–5:16	Ezek. 24:15–27; 33:7–22

Date	Psalm	Year A	Year B	Year C
1	85	Acts 24	Acts 5:17–42	Ezekiel 34
2	90	Acts 25	Acts 6	Ezek. 37:1–14
3	91	Acts 26	Acts 7:1–34	Ezek. 37:15–28
4	92	Acts 27	Acts 7:35–8:1a	Ezek.40:1–4; 43:1–12
5	93, 150	Acts 28	Acts 8:1b–25	Ezek. 47:1–12
6	*The Transfiguration of our Lord – Holy Days (L) – Psalm 27 – 2 Corinthians 3:18–4:11*			
7	98, 99	Philippians 1:1–11	Tobit 1:3–20; 2:1–10	1 Macc. 1:1–15, 41–64
8	103	Phil. 1:12–30	Tob. 3:1–4:3, 20–21	2 Maccabees 6:12–31
9	104:1–24	Phil. 2:1–13	Tob. 5:1–6:1a	1 Macc. 2:15–48
10	104:24–35	Phil. 2:14–3:1a	Tob. 6:1b–18	1 Macc. 3:10–26
11	107:1–22	Phil. 3:1b–16	Tob. 7:1–8:5	1 Macc. 4:36–59
12	107:23–43	Phil. 3:17–4:1	Tob. 9:1–10:12	2 Macc. 12:32–45
13	110, 111	Phil. 4:2–9	Tob. 11	1 Macc. 6:1–13
14	119:1–24	Phil. 4:10–23	Tob. 12	1 Macc. 9:1–22
15	*The Blessed Virgin Mary – Saints (VM) – Psalm 45 – Ephesians 1:17–2:10*			
16	26, 30	Judges 2:6–23	2 Samuel 1:1–2:11	1 Kings 16:29–17:24
17	32, 36	Judg. 4:1–5:3	2 Sam. 5	1 Ki. 18:1, 17–40
18	114, 149	Judg. 6	2 Sam. 6	1 Ki. 18:41–19:21
19	95, 115	Judg. 7	2 Sam. 7	1 Ki. 21
20	116, 117	Judg. 9:1–24	2 Sam. 9	1 Ki. 22:1–38
21	121, 122, 123	Judg. 13	2 Sam. 11:1–25	2 Kings 2:1–18
22	126, 127	Judg. 14	2 Sam. 11:26–12:25	2 Ki. 5
23	130, 133, 134	Judg. 15:1–16:3	2 Sam. 15	2 Ki. 6:8–23
24	*St Bartholomew – Saints (AE) – Psalm 86 – John 1:43–51*			
25	137, 146	Judges 16:4–31	2 Sam. 16	2 Ki. 18:1–12
26	139	Ruth 1; 2	2 Sam. 17	2 Ki. 18:13–19:7
27	119:25–48	Ruth 3; 4	2 Sam. 18	2 Ki. 19:8–37
28	144	1 Samuel 1	2 Sam. 19:1–18a	2 Ki. 22
29	145	1 Sam. 2:12–26; 3	2 Sam. 19:18b–43	Jeremiah 19
30	147	1 Sam. 4	2 Sam. 23:1–17	Jer. 26:1–16
31	148	1 Sam. 5; 6:1–16	2 Sam. 24	Jer. 32

From 7–14 August the readings for Years B and C are from books which some Bibles place in the Apocrypha.

If this is not available, use the readings for Year A.

Date	Psalm	Year A	Year B	Year C
1	34	1 Sam. 8	1 Ki. 1:11–40; 2:10–11	2 Kings 24:18–25:21
2	1, 4, 6	1 Sam. 9:1–26a	1 Kings 3:1–15	Jeremiah 24
3	12, 16	1 Sam. 9:26b–10:24	1 Ki. 3:16–28; 4:20–25	Jer. 29:1–14
4	19	1 Sam. 13:1–14	1 Ki. 4:29–34; 6:1–14	Nehemiah 1:1–2:8
5	23, 32	1 Sam. 16	1 Ki. 8:1–21	Neh. 2:9–20
6	25	1 Sam. 17:1–40	1 Ki. 8:22–53	Neh. 4
7	28, 30	1 Sam. 17:41–18:16	1 Ki. 8:62–9:9	Neh. 5
8	119:49–72	1 Sam. 20	1 Ki. 10:1–13	Neh. 6:1–16
9	31	1 Sam. 21:1–10; 23:14–18	1 Ki. 11:1–13, 41–43	Neh. 8
10	35	1 Sam. 24	Galatians 1:1–10	Job 28
11	36, 46	1 Sam. 28	Gal. 1:11–24	2 Peter 1
12	37:1–20	Titus 1:1–2:10	Gal. 2:1–14	2 Pet. 2
13	37:21–40	Titus 2:11–3:15	Gal. 2:15–21	2 Pet. 3
14		*Holy Cross Day – Holy Days (L) – Psalms 3, 8 – John 12:27–36a*		
15	42, 43	Hosea 1; 3	Gal. 3:1–14	Amos 1:1–2; 2:4–16
16	51	Hos. 2:2, 8–23	Gal. 3:15–29	Amos 3:1–4:5
17	55	Hos. 6:1–6; 10:1–4	Gal. 4:1–20	Amos 5:1–24
18	56	Hos. 11:1–11	Gal. 4:21–31	Amos 7
19	57	Hos. 13	Gal. 5	Amos 8:4–14
20	61, 62	Hos. 14	Gal. 6	Amos 9:5–15
21		*St Matthew – Saints (AE) – Psalm 49 – 1 Timothy 6:6–19*		
22	119:81–104	Matthew 1:18–2:23	Ecclesiastes 1	Luke 1:1–4; 3:1–22
23	63, 93	Matt. 3:1–4:22	Eccles. 2	Luke 4:1–30
24	65, 150	Matt. 4:23–5:20	Eccles. 3	Luke 4:31–5:11
25	66	Matt. 5:21–48	Eccles. 4:1–5:9	Luke 5:12–6:5
26	67, 98	Matt. 6	Eccles. 5:10–6:12	Luke 6:6–26
27	116, 117	Matt. 7	Eccles. 7	Luke 6:27–49
28	145	Matt. 8:1–9:1	Eccles. 8:5–9:10	Luke 7:1–35
29		*St Michael and All Angels – Holy Days (L) – Psalm 34 – 2 Kings 6:8–17*		
30	77	Matt. 9:2–34	Eccles. 11	Luke 7:36–8:8

Date	Psalm	Year A	Year B	Year C
1	80	Matt. 9:35–10:42	Eccles. 12	Luke 8:9–25
2	81	Matt. 11	Mark 1:1–28	Luke 8:26–56
3	84	Matt. 12:1–21	Mark 1:29–2:12	Luke 9:1–27
4	85	Matt. 12:22–50	Mark 2:13–3:6	Luke 9:28–50
5	119:105–128	Matt. 13:1–23	Mark 3:7–35	Luke 9:51–10:24
6	104:1–24	Matt. 13:24–53	Mark 4:1–34	Luke 10:25–42
7	104:24–35	Matt. 13:54–14:21	Mark 4:35–5:20	Luke 11:1–28
8	86	Matt. 14:22–15:28	Mark 5:21–6:6a	Luke 11:29–54
9	90	Matt. 15:29–16:12	Mark 6:6b–29	Luke 12:1–34
10	91	Matt. 16:13–17:13	Mark 6:30–56	Luke 12:35–59
11	92	Matt. 17:14–27	Mark 7:1–23	Luke 13
12	95, 113	Matt. 18	Mark 7:24–8:21	Luke 14
13	99, 114	Matt. 19	Mark 8:22–9:1	Luke 15
14	103	Matt. 20	Mark 9:2–29	Luke 16
15	107:1–22	Matt. 21:1–27	Mark 9:30–50	Luke 17:1–19
16	107:23–43	Matt. 21:28–22:14	Mark 10:1–31	Luke 17:20–18:14
17	119:129–152	Matt. 22:15–46	Mark 10:32–52	Luke 18:15–43
18		St Luke – Saints (AE) – Psalm 145 – James 5:13–16		
19	115	Matt. 23	Mark 11:1–25	Luke 19:1–27
20	118	Matt. 24:1–44	Mark 11:27–12:17	Luke 19:28–20:8
21	121, 122	Matt. 24:45–25:30	Mark 12:18–44	Luke 20:9–21:4
22	124, 142	Matt. 25:31–46	Mark 13	Luke 21:5–36
23	130, 131, 134	Matt. 26:1–35	Mark 14:1–31	Luke 21:37–22:38
24	135	Matt. 26:36–75	Mark 14:32–72	Luke 22:39–71
25	136	Matt. 27:1–26	Mark 15:1–39	Luke 23:1–25
26	139	Matt. 27:27–66	Mark 15:40–16:8	Luke 23:26–56
27	146	Matt. 28	Mark 16:9–20	Luke 24
28		St Simon and St Jude – Saints (AE) – Psalm 116 – Isaiah 45:18–25		
29	147	Haggai 1	Zechariah 8	Malachi 1:6–14
30	148	Hag. 2	Zech. 11:4–17	Mal. 3:1–4:6
31	119:153–176	Zephaniah 3:9–18	Zech. 13:1–6; 14:16–21	Micah 4:1–7; 7:18–20

Continue with The Season of Joyful Hope.

Date	Psalm	Scripture	
1	All Saints – Saints (AE) – Psalms 15, 84 – Revelation 19:5–10		
2	All Souls – use Monday texts – Psalm 27 – Romans 14:7–9		
3	2	Isaiah 6	
4	3, 14	Isa. 1:1–20	
5	5	Isa. 4:2–5:7	
6	19	Isa. 7:1–17	
7	21	Isa. 10:33–11:9	
8	29	Isa. 24	
9	33	Isa. 25:6–26:19	
10	44	Isa. 27:2–13	The Season of Joyful Hope
11	46	Isa. 33:1–22	
12	49	Isa. 40	
13	50	Isa. 41:1–20	
14	52, 53	Isa. 42:1–17	
15	57, (58)	Isa. 43:1–21	
16	59	Isa. 44:1–23	
17	66	Isa. 49:1–16,22–26	
18	67, 93	Isa. 50:4–51:8	
19	74	Isa. 54	
The Sunday before Advent (between 20 and 26 November)			
Christ the King – Holy Days (L) – Psalms 29, 110 – Revelation 11:15–19			
20	76	Isa. 58:1–12	
21	80	Isa. 62	
22	83	Isa.66:1–2,10–14,22–24	
23	97	1 Thess. 1:1–2:12	
24	99	1 Thess. 2:13–3:13	The Season of Joyful Hope
25	125, 126	1 Thessalonians 4	
26	144	1 Thess. 5	
27	146	2 Thess. 1	
28	1, (109)	2 Thess. 2	
29	7	2 Thess. 3	
30	St Andrew – Saints (AE) – Psalms 46, 47 – John 1:35–42		

Note – If 30 Nov. is the First Sunday of Advent,
use the psalm and reading for 1 Dec. on that day and keep St Andrew on the Monday.

DECEMBER — THE SEASON OF JOYFUL HOPE (Page 19)

Date	Psalm	Scripture	
1	9	Luke 1:5–25, 57–66	
2	10	Luke 3:1–20	
3	11, 12	Matthew 9:35–10:15	
4	24	Matt. 10:16–33	
5	62	Matt. 11:1–24	
6	64	Matt. 13:24–52	
7	70, 82	Luke 12:13–31	
8	75	Luke 12:32–40	The Season of Joyful Hope
9	94	Luke 12:41–56	
10	98	Mark 13:1–23	
11	102	Mark 13:24–37	
12	106:1–23	Daniel 1:1–2:16	
13	106:24–48	Dan. 2:17–49	
14	123, 137	Dan. 3	
15	129, 149	Dan. 5	
16	130, 141	Dan. 6	

THE SEASON OF THE WORD MADE FLESH (Page 31)

Date	Psalm	Scripture	
17	148	1 John 1:1–7	
18	144	1 John 1:8–2:11	
19	132	1 John 2:12–17	
20	114	1 John 2:18–3:3	The Season of the Word Made Flesh
21	81	1 John 3:4–24	
22	67, 87	1 John 4:1–5:4	
23	27	1 John 5:5–21	
24	85	Micah 5:2–5a	
25		Christmas Day – use Sunday texts – Psalms 110, 111 – Matthew 1:18–25	
26		St Stephen – Saints (M) – Psalms 13, 31:2–9 – Acts 6	
27		St John the Evangelist – Saints (AE) – Psalm 21 – Revelation 21	
28		Holy Innocents – Saints (M) – Psalms 8, 36 – Matthew 18:1–10	
29		St Thomas Becket – Saints (M) – Psalm 11 – 2 Timothy 2:3–13	
30	84	Hebrews 4:14–5:10	The Season of the Word Made Flesh
31	90	Heb. 5:11–6:20	

SUPPLEMENTARY MATERIAL
FOR SAINTS AND HOLY DAYS (Page 93)

The following Festivals do not have a specific calendar date.

Psalm	Scripture	
33	Genesis 1:1–5	*Trinity Sunday*
		The Sunday after Pentecost – Holy Days (L)
147	John 6:22–35	*Corpus Christi*
		The Thursday after Trinity Sunday – Holy Days (L)
23	John 19:31–37	*Sacred Heart*
		Friday, the week after Corpus Christi – Holy Days (L)
48	1 Corinthians 3:9–17	*Dedication Festival*
		Saints (AE or category of the Saint)

Many people will wish to keep Saints' Days other than those listed in the monthly calendars.
Decide which of these categories the saint best falls into and use one of the sets of
Psalms and Readings from the table below.

Psalm	Scripture	Category of Saint
87	Isaiah 52:7–10	*Apostles and Evangelists (AE)*
97	Matthew 28:16–20	
45	Acts 1:12–14	*Virgin Mary (VM)*
131, 138	Luke 11:27–28	
3, 11	1 Corinthians 4:8–13	*Martyrs (M)*
126	Isaiah 43:1–7	
34	Malachi 2:4–7	*Pastors (P)*
110	2 Timothy 4:1–8	
32	2 Corinthians 4:5–7	*Others (O)*
139:1–18	Micah 6:6–8	

DAILY PRAYER

The Season of Joyful Hope

1 November
until
16 December
inclusive.

After that turn to
The Season of the Word Made Flesh
on page 31.

OPENING

V. The kingdom of God is at hand:
R. **Come, let us worship.**

Invitatory: Psalm 96:1–2a, 10–13

O sing a new song to the Lord,
sing to the Lord all the earth.
O sing to the Lord, bless his name.

Proclaim to the nations: 'God is king.'
The world was made firm in its place;
God will judge the people in fairness.

Let the heavens rejoice and earth be glad,
let the sea and all within it thunder praise,
let the land and all it bears rejoice,
all the trees of the wood shout for joy

at the presence of the Lord who comes,
who comes to rule the earth:
comes with justice to rule the world,
and to judge the peoples with truth.

Give praise to the Father almighty,
to his Son, Jesus Christ, the Lord,
to the Spirit who dwells in our hearts,
both now and for ever. Amen.

Alleluia!

A hymn, or this, or another acclamation may be sung

Wait for the Lord, whose day is near.
Wait for the Lord: keep watch, take heart!

Opening Prayer

Blessed are you, Sovereign God,
ruler and judge of all,
to you be praise and glory for ever.

A few words of extempore prayer may be added here

Awaken in us joyful hope
as we look for Christ's reign of peace,
when every voice shall give you praise,
Father, Son, and Holy Spirit.

Blessed be God for ever!

Daily Prayer continues on the following pages according to the day.

SUNDAY

The psalm(s) are said. See Lectionary tables (pages 16–17).

Canticle of the Day: A Song of the Church (Te Deum)

We praise you, O God,
we acclaim you as Lord;
all creation worships you,
the Father everlasting.

To you all angels, all the powers of heaven,
the cherubim and seraphim, sing in endless praise:

Holy, holy, holy Lord,
God of power and might,
heaven and earth are full of your glory.

The glorious company of apostles praise you.
The noble fellowship of prophets praise you.

The white-robed army of martyrs praise you.
Throughout the world the holy Church acclaims you:

Father, of majesty unbounded,
your true and only Son, worthy of all praise,
the Holy Spirit, advocate and guide.

You, Christ, are the king of glory,
the eternal Son of the Father.

When you took our flesh to set us free
you humbly chose the Virgin's womb.
You overcame the sting of death
and opened the kingdom of heaven to all believers.

You are seated at God's right hand in glory.
We believe that you will come to be our judge.

Come then, Lord, and help your people,
bought with the price of your own blood,
and bring us with your saints to glory everlasting.

The Scripture Reading is read. See Lectionary tables (pages 16–17).

The Responsory (from Isaiah 60:20, 19)

V. The Lord will be your everlasting light.
R. **The Lord will be your everlasting light.**
V. Your God will be your glory;
R. **your everlasting light.**
V. Glory to the Father, the Son, the Holy Spirit.
R. **The Lord will be your everlasting light.**

Daily Prayer continues with the Canticle of the Season on page 28.

MONDAY

The psalm(s) are said. See Lectionary tables (pages 16–17).

Canticle of the Day:
A Song of the Wilderness (Isaiah 35:1, 2b, 3–4a, 5–7a, 10)

> The wilderness and the dry land shall rejoice,
> the desert shall blossom and burst into song.
> They shall see the glory of the Lord,
> the majesty of our God.
>
> Strengthen the weary hands,
> and make firm the feeble knees.
> Say to the anxious,
> 'Be strong, fear not,
> your God is coming with judgement;
> coming with judgement to save you.'
>
> Then shall the eyes of the blind be opened
> and the ears of the deaf unstopped;
> then shall the lame leap like a hart
> and the tongue of the dumb sing for joy.
>
> For waters shall break forth in the wilderness
> and streams in the desert.
>
> The ransomed of the Lord shall return with singing,
> with everlasting joy upon their heads.
> Joy and gladness shall be theirs,
> and sorrow and sighing shall flee away.
>
> Give praise to the Father . . .

The Scripture Reading is read. See Lectionary tables (pages 16–17).

The Responsory (from Isaiah 40:31)

> V. Those who wait for the Lord shall renew their strength.
> R. **Those who wait for the Lord shall renew their strength.**
> V. They shall mount up with wings like eagles;
> R. **they shall renew their strength.**
> V. Glory to the Father, the Son, the Holy Spirit.
> R. **Those who wait for the Lord shall renew their strength.**

Daily Prayer continues with the Canticle of the Season on page 28.

TUESDAY

The psalm(s) are said. See Lectionary tables (pages 16–17).

Canticle of the Day: A Song of the Lord's Return (Isaiah 52:7–10).

> How lovely on the mountains
> are the feet of those
> who bring good news.
>
> Who announce peace,
> who proclaim salvation,
> who say to Zion,
> 'Your God reigns.'
>
> Listen!
> Your watchmen lift up their voices,
> together they shout for joy;
> for with their own eyes they see
> the return of the Lord to Zion.
>
> Break forth together into singing,
> you ruins of Jerusalem,
> for the Lord has comforted his people.
>
> The Lord has bared his holy arm
> before the eyes of all the nations,
> and all the ends of the earth shall see
> the salvation of our God.
>
> Give praise to the Father . . .

The Scripture Reading is read. See Lectionary tables (pages 16–17).

The Responsory (from Isaiah 64:1, 2)
> V. O that you would tear open the heavens.
> R. **O that you would tear open the heavens.**
> V. Make your name known to your adversaries,
> R. **tear open the heavens.**
> V. Glory to the Father, the Son, the Holy Spirit.
> R. **O that you would tear open the heavens.**

Daily Prayer continues with the Canticle of the Season on page 28.

WEDNESDAY

The psalm(s) are said. See Lectionary tables (pages 16–17).

Canticle of the Day:
A Song of the Lamb (Revelation 19:1b, 5b, 6b–7, 9b)

> Salvation and glory and power
> belong to our God
> whose judgements are true and just.

> Praise our God
> all you servants of God,
> you who fear him
> both small and great.

> The Lord our God
> the Almighty reigns.
> Let us rejoice and exult
> and give glory and homage.

> The marriage of the Lamb has come
> and his bride has made herself ready.
> Happy are those who are invited
> to the wedding banquet of the Lamb.

> To the One who sits on the throne
> and to the Lamb
> be blessing and honour
> and glory and might,
> for ever and ever. Amen.

The Scripture Reading is read. See Lectionary tables (pages 16–17).

The Responsory (from Isaiah 45:2)

V. I will go before you; I will level the mountains.
R. **I will go before you; I will level the mountains.**
V. I will cut through the bars of iron;
R. **I will level the mountains.**
V. Glory to the Father, the Son, the Holy Spirit.
R. **I will go before you; I will level the mountains.**

Daily Prayer continues with the Canticle of the Season on page 28.

THURSDAY

The psalm(s) are said. See Lectionary tables (pages 16–17).

Canticle of the Day:
A Song of God's Gladness (from Zephaniah 3:14–20)

> Sing aloud, O daughter of Zion,
> rejoice and exult with all your heart!
> The Lord has taken away
> the judgements against you;
> you shall fear disaster no more.

> The Lord your God is in your midst,
> a warrior who gives victory:
> he will rejoice over you with gladness,
> he will renew you in his love,
> he will exult over you with loud singing
> as on a day of festival.

> 'I will deal with all your oppressors at that time,'
> says the Lord.
> 'I will bring you home
> and restore your fortunes before your eyes.
> I will save the lame and gather the outcast;
> I will change their shame
> into praise and renown in all the earth.'

> Give praise to the Father . . .

The Scripture Reading is read. See Lectionary tables (pages 16–17).

The Responsory (from Isaiah 43:1)

V.   Do not fear, for I have redeemed you.
R.   **Do not fear, for I have redeemed you.**
V.   I have called you by name, you are mine;
R.   **I have redeemed you.**
V.   Glory to the Father, the Son, the Holy Spirit.
R.   **Do not fear, for I have redeemed you.**

Daily Prayer continues with the Canticle of the Season on page 28.

FRIDAY

The psalm(s) are said. See Lectionary tables (pages 16–17).

Canticle of the Day: A Song of Salvation (Henry Allon)

Jesus, Saviour of the world,
come to us in your mercy:
we look to you to save and help us.

By your cross and your life laid down,
you set your people free:
we look to you to save and help us.

When they were ready to perish,
you saved your disciples:
we look to you to come to our help.

In the greatness of your mercy,
loose us from our chains:
forgive the sins of all your people.

Make yourself known
as our saviour and mighty deliverer:
save and help us that we may praise you.

Come now and dwell with us,
Lord Christ Jesus:
hear our prayer and be with us always.

And when you come in your glory,
make us to be one with you
and to share the life of your kingdom.

The Scripture Reading is read. See Lectionary tables (pages 16–17).

The Responsory (from Isaiah 66:13, 11)

V.   As a mother comforts her child, so I will comfort you.
R.   **As a mother comforts her child, so I will comfort you.**
V.   Drink deeply with delight,
R.   **I will comfort you.**
V.   Glory to the Father, the Son, the Holy Spirit.
R.   **As a mother comforts her child, so I will comfort you.**

Daily Prayer continues with the Canticle of the Season on page 28.

SATURDAY

The psalm(s) are said. See Lectionary tables (pages 16–17).

Canticle of the Day: A Song of Peace (Isaiah 2:3–5)

> Come, let us go up to the mountain of God
> to the house of the God of Jacob;
> that God may teach us his ways
> and that we may walk in his paths;
> for the law shall go out from Zion,
> and the word of the Lord from Jerusalem.
>
> God shall mediate between the nations
> and shall judge for many peoples.
> They shall beat their swords into ploughshares
> and their spears into pruning hooks.
>
> Nation shall not lift up sword against nation,
> neither shall they learn war any more.
>
> O people of Jacob, come,
> let us walk in the light of the Lord.
>
> Give praise to the Father . . .

The Scripture Reading is read. See Lectionary tables (pages 16–17).

The Responsory (from Isaiah 60:2)

> V. Darkness shall cover the earth, but the Lord will rise upon you.
> R. **Darkness shall cover the earth, but the Lord will rise upon you.**
> V. His glory shall appear over you,
> R. **the Lord will rise upon you.**
> V. Glory to the Father, the Son, the Holy Spirit.
> R. **Darkness shall cover the earth, but the Lord will rise upon you.**

Daily Prayer continues with the Canticle of the Season on page 28.

EVERY DAY

CANTICLE OF THE SEASON

The Song of Zechariah (Luke 1:68–79)

Blessed be the Lord, the God of Israel,
who has come to his people and set them free.
The Lord has raised up for us a mighty Saviour,
born of the house of his servant David.

Through the holy prophets, God promised of old
to save us from our enemies,
from the hands of all who hate us,
to show mercy to our forebears,
and to remember his holy covenant.

This was the oath God swore to our father Abraham:
to set us free from the hands of our enemies,
free to worship him without fear,
holy and righteous before him,
all the days of our life.

And you, child, shall be called the prophet of the Most High,
for you will go before the Lord to prepare his way,
to give his people knowledge of salvation
by the forgiveness of their sins.

In the tender compassion of our God
the dawn from on high shall break upon us,
to shine on those who dwell in darkness and the shadow of death,
and to guide our feet into the way of peace.

Give praise to the Father almighty,
to his Son, Jesus Christ, the Lord,
to the Spirit who dwells in our hearts,
both now and for ever. Amen.

PRAYER AND THANKSGIVING

The Lord's Prayer is said. It may be introduced by

> Looking to the coming of God's kingdom, we pray:
> Our Father . . .

Specific intercessions and thanksgivings should be offered here.

These may begin with:

Today	its encounters, opportunities and demands.
Currently	concerns and achievements in our churches and society: locally, nationally and around the world.

A personal Prayer Diary or some other Cycle of Intercession may guide further prayer.

Prayer may also be offered using one or more of the following categories:

Local	Community life, work, leisure, education.
	The sick, the bereaved, the lonely.
	The witness and fellowship of God's people.
National	Government, commerce and industry, institutions.
	The unemployed, victims of crime, or marginalised.
	The Church: its leaders and its prophetic role.
Global	Nations and their leaders; justice, peace and development.
	Refugees and victims of war.
	The dispossessed, the hungry, the persecuted.
	The Church: its partnership in world mission.

The period of prayer is concluded with the following responses:

> V. In joyful hope we pray to you, O Lord:
> R. **come, Lord Jesus.**
>
> V. Come to your Church as Lord and Judge:
> R. **give us a longing for your loving rule.**
>
> V. Come to your world as King of the nations:
> R. **let righteousness and peace prevail.**
>
> V. Come to us as Saviour and Comforter:
> R. **break into our failure and free us to serve you.**
>
> V. Come to us with power and great glory:
> R. **lift up our hearts to meet you in joy.**

The collect of the day should be said if available.

One or more of these Concluding Prayers is said, or another of your choice:

Gracious Father,
by whose tender compassion
the light of Christ has dawned upon us:
> open our hearts,
> so that, joyfully receiving Christ,
> we may declare his glory to the ends of the earth.
He lives and reigns with you and the Holy Spirit,
one God, for ever and ever. **Amen.**

God our Father,
> by your command the order of time runs its course;
forgive our impatience, perfect our faith,
and, while we wait for the fulfilment of your promises,
grant us to have a good hope because of your word;
> through Jesus Christ our Lord. **Amen.**

Reveal in us your glory, Lord,
> stir in us your power.
Renew in us your kingdom, Lord,
> strengthen in us your hope.
Work in us your miracles, Lord,
> abide in us yourself. **Amen.**

As we wait in hope for your coming reign,
> God, grant us
> the serenity to accept the things we cannot change,
> courage to change the things we can,
> and wisdom to know the difference;
that your peace may guard our hearts and minds
in Christ Jesus. **Amen.**

CONCLUSION

May the God of hope fill us with all joy and peace in believing, so that we may abound in hope by the power of the Holy Spirit. Amen.

DAILY PRAYER

The Season
of
The Word Made Flesh

17 December
until
2 February

After that turn to
Through the Year
on page 81
until Shrove Tuesday.

OPENING

V. The Word was made flesh and lived among us:

R. **Come, let us worship.**

Invitatory: Psalm 98:1–4

Sing a new song to the Lord
who has worked wonders;
whose right hand and holy arm
have brought salvation.

The Lord has made known salvation;
has shown justice to the nations;
has remembered truth and love
for the house of Israel.

All the ends of the earth have seen
the salvation of our God.
Shout to the Lord, all the earth,
ring out your joy.

Give praise to the Father almighty,
to his Son, Jesus Christ, the Lord,
to the Spirit who dwells in our hearts,
both now and for ever. Amen.

Alleluia!

A hymn, or this, or another acclamation may be sung

Jesus, Name above all names,
beautiful Saviour, glorious Lord,
Emmanuel, God is with us,
blessed Redeemer, living Word.

Opening Prayer

Blessed are you, Christ our Lord,
our everlasting light
and redeemer of the world.

A few words of extempore prayer may be added here

By taking upon yourself our mortal nature
you saved humanity
and restored joy to the whole world.

Blessed be God for ever!

Daily Prayer continues on the following pages according to the day.

SUNDAY

The psalm(s) are said. See Lectionary tables (pages 17 and 4).

Canticle of the Day: A Song of the Messiah (Isaiah 9:2–7)

> The people who walked in darkness
> have seen a great light;
> those who dwelt in a land of deep darkness,
> upon them the light has dawned.
>
> You have increased their joy
> and given them great gladness;
> they rejoiced before you as with joy at the harvest.
> For you have shattered the yoke that burdened them;
> the collar that lay heavy on their shoulders.
>
> For to us a child is born and to us a son is given,
> and the government will be upon his shoulder.
>
> And his name will be called:
> Wonderful Counsellor;
> the Mighty God;
> the Everlasting Father;
> the Prince of Peace.
>
> Of the increase of his government and of peace
> there will be no end,
> upon the throne of David and over his kingdom.
>
> To establish and uphold it with justice and righteousness
> from this time forth and for evermore.
> The zeal of the Lord of hosts will do this.
>
> Give praise to the Father . . .

The Scripture Reading is read. See Lectionary tables (pages 17 and 4).

The Responsory (from John 1:1, 4)

> V. In the beginning was the Word, the Word was with God.
> R. **In the beginning was the Word, the Word was with God.**
> V. The Word was the light,
> R. **the Word was with God.**
> V. Glory to the Father, the Son, the Holy Spirit.
> R. **In the beginning was the Word, the Word was with God.**

Daily Prayer continues with the Canticle of the Season on page 40.

MONDAY

The psalm(s) are said. See Lectionary tables (pages 17 and 4).

Canticle of the Day: A Song of Grace and Renewal (Titus 3:4–7)

When the goodness
and loving kindness
of God our Saviour appeared,
he saved us;

not because of any works
of righteousness that we had done,
but according to his mercy,
through the water of rebirth
and renewal by the Holy Spirit.

This Spirit he poured out on us richly
through Jesus Christ our Saviour,
so that, having been justified by his grace,
we might become heirs according to the hope of eternal life.

Give praise to the Father . . .

The Scripture Reading is read. See Lectionary tables (pages 17 and 4).

The Responsory (from 1 John 2:8, 10)

V.   The darkness is passing away; the true light is already shining.
R.   **The darkness is passing away; the true light is already shining.**
V.   Let us live in the light,
R.   **the true light is already shining.**
V.   Glory to the Father, the Son, the Holy Spirit.
R.   **The darkness is passing away; the true light is already shining.**

Daily Prayer continues with the Canticle of the Season on page 40.

TUESDAY

The psalm(s) are said. See Lectionary tables (pages 17 and 4).

Canticle of the Day:
A Song of the Gospel of God (from Romans 11:33–35; 1:1–7,16–17)

Who can measure
the wealth and wisdom and knowledge of God?

How unsearchable are his judgements
and how inscrutable his ways!

For who has known the mind of the Lord?
Or who has been his counsellor?
Who has given a gift to him,
to receive a gift in return?

The gospel of God,
which was promised beforehand through the prophets,
is the good news of the One
descended from David according to the flesh
and declared to be Son of God in power
by resurrection from the dead;

Jesus Christ our Lord,
through whom we have received grace
for the obedience of faith,
in whom we are called to be saints.

This gospel is the power of God for salvation
to everyone who has faith.
In it the righteousness of God is revealed;
by it, those who are righteous through faith will live.

The Scripture Reading is read. See Lectionary tables (pages 17 and 4).

The Responsory (from 1 John 4:14, 15)

> V. The Father has sent his Son as the Saviour of the world.
> R. **The Father has sent his Son as the Saviour of the world.**
> V. Jesus is the Son of God,
> R. **the Saviour of the world.**
> V. Glory to the Father, the Son, the Holy Spirit.
> R. **The Father has sent his Son as the Saviour of the world.**

Daily Prayer continues with the Canticle of the Season on page 40.

WEDNESDAY

The psalm(s) are said. See Lectionary tables (pages 17 and 4).

Canticle of the Day:
A Song of the New Jerusalem (Isaiah 60:1–3, 11, 18–19, 14)

> Arise, shine out, for your light has come,
> the glory of the Lord is rising upon you.

> Though night still covers the earth
> and darkness the peoples;
> above you the Holy One arises
> and above you God's glory appears.

> The nations will come to your light,
> and kings to your dawning brightness.

> Your gates will lie open continually,
> shut neither by day nor by night.
> The sound of violence shall be heard no longer in your land,
> or ruin and devastation within your borders.

> You will call your walls, Salvation,
> and your gates, Praise.

> No more will the sun give you daylight,
> nor moonlight shine upon you;
> but the Lord will be your everlasting light,
> your God will be your splendour.

> For you shall be called the city of God,
> the dwelling of the Holy One of Israel.

> Give praise to the Father . . .

The Scripture Reading is read. See Lectionary tables (pages 17 and 4).

The Responsory (from 1 John 5:11, 20)

> V.   God gave us eternal life, and this life is in his Son.
> R.   **God gave us eternal life, and this life is in his Son.**
> V.   He is the true God and eternal life,
> R.   **and this life is in his Son.**
> V.   Glory to the Father, the Son, the Holy Spirit.
> R.   **God gave us eternal life, and this life is in his Son.**

Daily Prayer continues with the Canticle of the Season on page 40.

THURSDAY

The psalm(s) are said. See Lectionary tables (pages 17 and 4).

Canticle of the Season:
A Song of God's Generosity (from James 1:16–18)

> All that is good,
> all that is perfect,
> is given to us from above.
>
> It comes down from the Father of all light
> with whom there is no shadow of change.
>
> By his own choice he gave birth to us
> by the message of truth
>
> so that we should be
> the first fruits of God's creation.
>
> Give praise to the Father . . .

The Scripture Reading is read. See Lectionary tables (pages 17 and 4).

The Responsory (from 1 John 4:7)

V.   Let us love one another, because love is from God.
R.   **Let us love one another, because love is from God.**
V.   Everyone who loves is born of God,
R.   **because love is from God.**
V.   Glory to the Father, the Son, the Holy Spirit.
R.   **Let us love one another, because love is from God.**

Daily Prayer continues with the Canticle of the Season on page 40.

FRIDAY

The psalm(s) are said. See Lectionary tables (pages 17 and 4).

Canticle of the Day: A Song of Redemption (Colossians 1:13–20)

The Father has delivered us
from the dominion of darkness,
and transferred us
to the kingdom of his beloved Son;
in whom we have redemption,
the forgiveness of our sins.

He is the image of the invisible God,
the first-born of all creation.
For in him all things were created,
in heaven and on earth,
visible and invisible.

All things were created
through him and for him,
he is before all things
and in him all things hold together.
He is the head of the body, the Church;
he is the beginning,
the first-born from the dead.

For it pleased God that in him
all fullness should dwell,
and through him
all things be reconciled to himself.

Give praise to the Father . . .

The Scripture Reading is read. See Lectionary tables (pages 17 and 4).

The Responsory (from John 3:16–17)

    V.   God so loved the world that he gave his only Son.
    R.   **God so loved the world that he gave his only Son.**
    V.   In order that the world might be saved,
    R.   **he gave his only Son.**
    V.   Glory to the Father, the Son, the Holy Spirit.
    R.   **God so loved the world that he gave his only Son.**

Daily Prayer continues with the Canticle of the Season on page 40.

SATURDAY

The psalm(s) are said. See Lectionary tables (pages 17 and 4).

Canticle of the Day:
A Song of Christ's Appearing (1 Timothy 3:16; 6:15–16)

> Christ Jesus was revealed in the flesh
> and vindicated in the spirit.
>
> He was seen by angels
> and proclaimed among the nations.
>
> Believed in throughout the world,
> he was taken up in glory.
>
> This will be made manifest at the proper time
> by the blessed and only Sovereign,
>
> who alone has immortality,
> and dwells in unapproachable light.
>
> To the King of kings and Lord of lords
> be honour and eternal dominion. Amen.

The Scripture Reading is read. See Lectionary tables (pages 17 and 4).

The Responsory (from John 6:68–69)

> V. You are the holy one of God, you have the words of eternal life.
> R. **You are the holy one of God, you have the words of eternal life.**
> V. Lord, to whom can we go,
> R. **you have the words of eternal life.**
> V. Glory to the Father, the Son, the Holy Spirit.
> R. **You are the holy one of God, you have the words of eternal life.**

Daily Prayer continues with the Canticle of the Season on page 40.

EVERY DAY

CANTICLE OF THE SEASON

The Song of Mary (Luke 1:46–55)

My soul proclaims the greatness of the Lord,
my spirit rejoices in God my Saviour,
who has looked with favour on his lowly servant.

From this day all generations will call me blessed:
the Almighty has done great things for me
and holy is his name.
God has mercy on those who fear him,
from generation to generation.

The Lord has shown strength with his arm
and scattered the proud in their conceit,
casting down the mighty from their thrones
and lifting up the lowly.

God has filled the hungry with good things
and sent the rich away empty.

He has come to the aid of his servant Israel,
to remember the promise of mercy,
the promise made to our forebears,
to Abraham and his children for ever.

Give praise to the Father almighty,
to his Son, Jesus Christ, the Lord,
to the Spirit who dwells in our hearts,
both now and for ever. Amen.

PRAYER AND THANKSGIVING

The Lord's Prayer is said. It may be introduced by

> Uniting earth with heaven, we pray:
> Our Father . . .

Specific intercessions and thanksgivings should be offered here.
These may begin with:

Today	its encounters, opportunities and demands.
Currently	concerns and achievements in our churches and society: locally, nationally and around the world.

A personal Prayer Diary or some other Cycle of Intercession may guide further prayer.

Prayer may also be offered using one or more of the following categories:

Local	Community life, work, leisure, education.
	The sick, the bereaved, the lonely.
	The witness and fellowship of God's people.
National	Government, commerce and industry, institutions.
	The unemployed, victims of crime, or marginalised.
	The Church: its leaders and its prophetic role.
Global	Nations and their leaders; justice, peace and development.
	Refugees and victims of war.
	The dispossessed, the hungry, the persecuted.
	The Church: its partnership in world mission.

The period of prayer is concluded with the following responses:

V.   Glory to God in the highest heaven:
R.   **goodwill to his people on earth.**

V.   Let the mountains be laden with peace:
R.   **and the hills with prosperity.**

V.   May righteousness flourish in our time:
R.   **your dominion stretch from sea to sea.**

V.   O God give justice to the poor:
R.   **deliver the needy when they cry.**

V.   For you alone do great wonders:
R.   **let the whole earth be filled with your glory.**

The collect of the day should be said if available.

One or more of these Concluding Prayers is said, or another of your choice:

Gracious Father,
your love for us shines forth in Christ,
    the Word made flesh.
Grant us his humble spirit,
that, recognising your presence
in those whose lives we touch,
we may honour you by serving them;
    through Jesus Christ our Lord. **Amen.**

O loving God,
you are the light of the minds that know you,
the life of the souls that love you,
and the strength of the hearts that serve you.
Help us so to know you that we may truly love you;
and so to love you that we may faithfully serve you,
whom to serve is perfect freedom;
through Jesus Christ our Lord. **Amen.**

Help us Lord:
    to live in your light,
    to act in your might,
    to think in your wisdom,
    to walk in your kingdom,
    to abide in your love;
    your presence to prove. **Amen.**

Today, O Lord, we say YES!
    to you,
        to life,
to all that is true, and good, and beautiful. **Amen.**

CONCLUSION

**May God, who has called us out of darkness into his wonderful
light, give us his peace and goodwill. Amen.**

DAILY PRAYER

The Season of Penitence

Ash Wednesday
until
the day before Palm Sunday.

Between *The Season of the Word Made Flesh* and *Ash Wednesday*
turn to *Through the Year* on page 81.

From *Palm Sunday* turn to
The Season of the Passion
on page 55.

OPENING

V. The Lord is full of compassion and mercy:

R. **Come, let us worship.**

Invitatory: Psalm 95:6–11

Come in; let us bow and bend low;
let us kneel before the God who made us
for this is our God and we
the people who belong to his pasture,
the flock that is led by his hand.

O that today you would listen to God's voice!
'Harden not your hearts as at Meribah,
as on that day at Massah in the desert
when your ancestors put me to the test;
when they tried me, though they saw my work.

For forty years I was wearied of these people
and I said: "Their hearts are astray,
these people do not know my ways."
Then I took an oath in my anger:
"Never shall they enter my rest."'

Give praise to the Father almighty,
to his Son, Jesus Christ, the Lord,
to the Spirit who dwells in our hearts,
both now and for ever. Amen.

A hymn, or this, or another acclamation may be sung

Do not be afraid, for I have redeemed you.
I have called you by your name; you are mine.

Opening Prayer

Blessed are you, holy God,
holy and strong, holy and immortal.

A few words of extempore prayer may be added here

Teach us to live in this passing world
with our hearts set on your eternal kingdom,
where, freed from sin and redeemed by your saving power,
we may praise and worship you for ever.

Blessed be God for ever!

Daily Prayer continues on the following pages according to the day.

SUNDAY

The psalm(s) are said. See Lectionary tables (pages 6–7).

Canticle of the Day: A Song of Creation (Song of the Three 35–65)

Bless the Lord all created things,
he is worthy to be praised and exalted for ever.
Bless the Lord you heavens,
he is worthy to be praised and exalted for ever.

Bless the Lord you angels of the Lord, bless the Lord all you his hosts,
bless the Lord you waters above the heavens,
he is worthy to be praised and exalted for ever.

Bless the Lord sun and moon, bless the Lord you stars of heaven,
bless the Lord all rain and dew,
he is worthy to be praised and exalted for ever.

Bless the Lord all winds that blow, bless the Lord you fire and heat,
bless the Lord scorching wind and bitter cold,
he is worthy to be praised and exalted for ever.

Bless the Lord dews and falling snows, bless the Lord you nights and days,
bless the Lord light and darkness,
he is worthy to be praised and exalted for ever.

Bless the Lord frost and cold, bless the Lord you ice and snow,
bless the Lord lightning and clouds,
he is worthy to be praised and exalted for ever.

O let the earth bless the Lord; bless the Lord you mountains and hills,
bless the Lord all that grows in the ground,
he is worthy to be praised and exalted for ever.

Bless the Lord you springs, bless the Lord you seas and rivers,
bless the Lord you whales and all that swim in the waters,
he is worthy to be praised and exalted for ever.

Bless the Lord all birds of the air, bless the Lord you beasts and cattle,
bless the Lord all people of the earth,
he is worthy to be praised and exalted for ever.

O People of God bless the Lord; bless the Lord you priests of the Lord,
bless the Lord you servants of the Lord,
he is worthy to be praised and exalted for ever.

Bless the Lord all you of upright spirit,
bless the Lord you that are holy and humble in heart.
Bless the Father, the Son, the Holy Spirit:
God, who is worthy to be praised and exalted for ever. Amen.

The Scripture Reading is read. See Lectionary tables (pages 6–7).

The Responsory (from Psalm 51:14, 20)

V. Save me, bring back my joy.
R. **Save me, bring back my joy.**
V. In your love make me lovely,
R. **bring back my joy.**
V. Glory to the Father, the Son, the Holy Spirit.
R. **Save me, bring back my joy.**

Daily Prayer continues with the Canticle of the Season on page 52.

MONDAY

The psalm(s) are said. See Lectionary tables (pages 6–7).

Canticle of the Day: A Song of the New Creation (Isaiah 43:15–21)

'I am the Lord, your Holy One,
the Creator of Israel, whom I have chosen.'

Thus says the Lord, who makes a way in the sea,
a path in the mighty waters,

'Remember not the former things,
nor consider the things of old.
Behold, I make all things new;
now it springs forth, do you not perceive it?

'I will make a way in the wilderness and rivers in the desert,
to give drink to my chosen people,
the people whom I formed for myself,
that they might declare my praise.'

Give praise to the Father . . .

The Scripture Reading is read. See Lectionary tables (pages 6–7).

The Responsory (from Psalm 51:9, 11)

V. Wash me with fresh water, wash me bright as snow.
R. **Wash me with fresh water, wash me bright as snow.**
V. Make my guilt disappear,
R. **wash me bright as snow.**
V. Glory to the Father, the Son, the Holy Spirit.
R. **Wash me with fresh water, wash me bright as snow.**

Daily Prayer continues with the Canticle of the Season on page 52.

TUESDAY

The psalm(s) are said. See Lectionary tables (pages 6–7).

Canticle of the Day: A Song of Christ the Servant (1 Peter 2:21–25)

Christ suffered for you,
leaving you an example
that you should follow in his steps.

He committed no sin,
no guile was found on his lips,
when he was reviled
he did not revile in turn.

When he suffered, he did not threaten,
but he trusted in God who judges justly.

Christ himself bore our sins
in his body on the tree,
that we might die to sin
and live to righteousness.

By his wounds you have been healed:
for you were straying like sheep
but have now returned
to the Shepherd and Guardian of your souls.

Give praise to the Father . . .

The Scripture Reading is read. See Lectionary tables (pages 6–7).

The Responsory (from Psalm 51:3, 4)

V.   Have mercy, tender God, forget that I defied you.
R.   **Have mercy, tender God, forget that I defied you.**
V.   Cleanse me from my guilt.
R.   **Forget that I defied you.**
V.   Glory to the Father, the Son, the Holy Spirit.
R.   **Have mercy, tender God, forget that I defied you.**

Daily Prayer continues with the Canticle of the Season on page 52.

WEDNESDAY

The psalm(s) are said. See Lectionary tables (pages 6–7).

Canticle of the Day: A Song of the Blessed (Matthew 5:3–12)

Blessed are the poor in spirit,
for theirs is the kingdom of heaven.

Blessed are those who mourn,
for they shall be comforted.

Blessed are the gentle,
for they shall inherit the earth.

Blessed are those who hunger and thirst for what is right,
for they shall be satisfied.

Blessed are the merciful,
for mercy shall be shown to them.

Blessed are the pure in heart,
for they shall see God.

Blessed are the peacemakers,
for they shall be called the children of God.

Blessed are those who are persecuted in the cause of right,
for theirs is the kingdom of heaven.

Blessed are you when others revile you and persecute you
and utter all kinds of evil against you falsely for my sake.

Rejoice and be glad
for your reward is great in heaven.

The Scripture Reading is read. See Lectionary tables (pages 6–7).

The Responsory (from Psalm 51:11, 10)

V.   Shut your eyes to my sin, make my guilt disappear.
R.   **Shut your eyes to my sin, make my guilt disappear.**
V.   Fill me with happy songs,
R.   **make my guilt disappear.**
V.   Glory to the Father, the Son, the Holy Spirit.
R.   **Shut your eyes to my sin, make my guilt disappear.**

Daily Prayer continues with the Canticle of the Season on page 52.

THURSDAY

The psalm(s) are said. See Lectionary tables (pages 6–7).

Canticle of the Day: A Song of God's Love (1 John 4:7–11)

> Beloved, let us love one another,
> for love is of God;
> everyone who loves
> is born of God and knows God.
>
> Whoever does not love
> does not know God,
> for God is love.
>
> In this the love of God was revealed among us,
> that God sent his only Son into the world
> so that we might live through him.
>
> In this is love,
> not that we loved God but that he loved us,
> and sent his Son to be the expiation for our sins.
>
> Beloved, since God loved us so much,
> we ought also to love one another.
>
> For if we love one another
> God abides in us,
> and God's love
> will be perfected in us.
>
> Give praise to the Father . . .

The Scripture Reading is read. See Lectionary tables (pages 6–7).

The Responsory (from Psalm 51:19, 12)

> V.   I offer my shattered spirit; a changed heart you welcome.
> R.   **I offer my shattered spirit; a changed heart you welcome.**
> V.   God, steady my spirit;
> R.   **a changed heart you welcome.**
> V.   Glory to the Father, the Son, the Holy Spirit.
> R.   **I offer my shattered spirit; a changed heart you welcome.**

Daily Prayer continues with the Canticle of the Season on page 52.

FRIDAY

The psalm(s) are said. See Lectionary tables (pages 6–7).

Canticle of the Day: A Song of the Servant (Isaiah 53:3–6)

He was despised, he was rejected,
a man of sorrows, acquainted with grief.
As one from whom people hide their faces
he was despised, and we did not esteem him.

He bore our sufferings,
he endured our torments,
while we thought he was being punished
and struck by God, brought low.

He was pierced for our sins,
bruised for no fault but our own.
His punishment has won our peace,
and by his wounds we are healed.

We have all strayed like sheep
each taking their own way.
But the Lord has laid on him
the guilt of us all.

Give praise to the Father . . .

The Scripture Reading is read. See Lectionary tables (pages 6–7).

The Responsory (from Psalm 51:4, 7)

V. Wash away my sin, cleanse me from my guilt.
R. **Wash away my sin, cleanse me from my guilt.**
V. You see me for what I am,
R. **cleanse me from my guilt.**
V. Glory to the Father, the Son, the Holy Spirit.
R. **Wash away my sin, cleanse me from my guilt.**

Daily Prayer continues with the Canticle of the Season on page 52.

SATURDAY

The psalm(s) are said. See Lectionary tables (pages 6–7).

Canticle of the Day:
A Song of the Word of the Lord (Isaiah 55:6–11)

   Seek the Lord while he is still to be found,
   call out to him while he is still near.

   Let the wicked abandon their ways
   and the evil their thoughts;
   let them turn back to the Lord
   who will have mercy on them,
   to God, who is rich in forgiveness.

   For my thoughts are not your thoughts, says the Lord,
   and my ways are not your ways.
   For as the heavens are higher than the earth,
   so are my ways higher than your ways,
   and my thoughts higher than your thoughts.

   For as the rain and the snow come down from the sky
   and do not return until they have watered the earth,
   giving it life and making the crops grow,
   providing seed to sow and food to eat,

   so with the word that goes from my mouth:
   it will not return to me unfulfilled,
   but will accomplish what I intend
   and succeed in what it was sent to do.

   Give praise to the Father . . .

The Scripture Reading is read. See Lectionary tables (pages 6–7).

The Responsory (from Psalm 51:16, 8)

   V.   Help me, stop my tears, and I will sing your goodness.
   R.   **Help me, stop my tears, and I will sing your goodness.**
   V.   Teach me your hidden wisdom,
   R.   **and I will sing your goodness.**
   V.   Glory to the Father, the Son, the Holy Spirit.
   R.   **Help me, stop my tears, and I will sing your goodness.**

Daily Prayer continues with the Canticle of the Season on page 52.

EVERY DAY

CANTICLE OF THE SEASON

A Song of Salvation (Henry Allon)

Jesus, Saviour of the world,
come to us in your mercy:
we look to you to save and help us.

By your cross and your life laid down,
you set your people free:
we look to you to save and help us.

When they were ready to perish,
you saved your disciples:
we look to you to come to our help.

In the greatness of your mercy,
loose us from our chains:
forgive the sins of all your people.

Make yourself known
as our saviour and mighty deliverer:
save and help us that we may praise you.

Come now and dwell with us,
Lord Christ Jesus:
hear our prayer and be with us always.

And when you come in your glory,
make us to be one with you
and to share the life of your kingdom.

PRAYER AND THANKSGIVING

The Lord's Prayer is said. It may be introduced by

> Looking to the Lord for our daily bread, we pray:
> Our Father . . .

Specific intercessions and thanksgivings should be offered here.

These may begin with:

Today	its encounters, opportunities and demands.
Currently	concerns and achievements in our churches and society: locally, nationally and around the world.

A personal Prayer Diary or some other Cycle of Intercession may guide further prayer.

Prayer may also be offered using one or more of the following categories:

Local	Community life, work, leisure, education.
	The sick, the bereaved, the lonely.
	The witness and fellowship of God's people.
National	Government, commerce and industry, institutions.
	The unemployed, victims of crime, or marginalised.
	The Church: its leaders and its prophetic role.
Global	Nations and their leaders; justice, peace and development.
	Refugees and victims of war.
	The dispossessed, the hungry, the persecuted.
	The Church: its partnership in world mission.

The period of prayer is concluded with the following responses:

> V. Save your people, Lord, and bless your inheritance:
> R. **govern and uphold them now and always.**

> V. Day by day we bless you:
> R. **we praise your name for ever.**

> V. Keep us today, Lord, from all sin:
> R. **have mercy on us, Lord, have mercy.**

> V. Lord, show us your love and mercy:
> R. **for we have put our trust in you.**

> V. In you, Lord, is our hope:
> R. **let us never be put to shame.**

The collect of the day should be said if available.

One or more of these Concluding Prayers is said, or another of your choice:

God of compassion,
    through your Son Jesus Christ
    you have reconciled your people to yourself.
As we follow his example of prayer and fasting,
    may we obey you with willing hearts
    and serve one another in holy love;
    through Jesus Christ our Lord. **Amen.**

Lord Jesus, we thank you
    for all the benefits you have won for us,
    for all the pains and insults you have borne for us.
Most merciful redeemer,
friend and brother,
    may we know you more clearly,
    love you more dearly,
    and follow you more nearly,
    day by day. **Amen.**

God of life, do not darken your light to us,
God of life, do not close your joy to us,
God of life, do not shut your door to us,
God of life, do not refuse your mercy to us,
God of life, crown us with your gladness. **Amen.**

O Christ the Light,
    illuminate and cleanse the dark corners of the world,
    where hang the cobwebs of apathy
    and the dust of neglect.
Shine on faces made grim by poverty and war;
    melt the icicles of despair,
    and the hard frozen wastes of selfishness;
and let your searching rays
enclose the whole in one great radiance. **Amen.**

CONCLUSION

**May Christ give us grace to grow in holiness, to deny ourselves, take up
our cross, and follow him. Amen.**

DAILY PRAYER

The Season
of
The Passion

Palm Sunday
until
Holy Saturday.

After that turn to
The Season of the Resurrection
on page 63.

During Holy Week, apart from the psalms and readings, the only variant is the Canticle of the Day, so *Daily Prayer* is set out in a slightly different format from the other seasons. Follow the order straight through, turning to the appropriate canticle for each day.

OPENING

V. Christ was obedient, even unto death:
R. **Come, let us worship.**

Invitatory: A Song of Humility (Hosea 6:1–6)

Come, let us return to the Lord,
who has torn us and will heal us.
God has stricken us,
and will bind up our wounds.

After two days, he will revive us,
and on the third day will raise us up
that we may live in his presence.

Let us humble ourselves,
let us strive to know our God,
whose justice dawns like the morning star,
its dawning is as sure as the sunrise.

God's justice will come to us like the showers,
like the spring rains that water the earth.

'O Ephraim, how shall I deal with you?
How shall I deal with you, O Jacob?
Your love for me is like the morning mist,
like the dew that goes early away.

'Therefore, I have hewn them by the prophets
and my judgement goes forth as the light.
For loyalty is my desire and not sacrifice,
and the knowledge of God rather than burnt offerings.'

Give praise to the Father almighty,
to his Son, Jesus Christ, the Lord,
to the Spirit who dwells in our hearts,
both now and for ever. Amen.

A hymn, or this, or another acclamation may be sung

Jesus, remember me
when you come into your kingdom.

Opening Prayer

We adore you, Christ, and we bless you,
because by your cross you have redeemed the world.

A few words of extempore prayer may be added here

Strengthen us to take up our cross every day
and follow you in the way that leads to eternal life.

Blessed be God for ever!

The psalm(s) are said. See Lectionary tables (page 8).

Canticle of the Day
This varies according to the day of the week as follows.

PALM SUNDAY

A Song of the Redeemer (Isaiah 63:1–3a, 7–9)

Who is this that comes from Edom,
coming from Bozrah, his garments stained crimson?
Who is this, in glorious apparel,
marching in the greatness of his strength?

'It is I, who announce that right has won the day.
It is I,' says the Lord, 'for I am mighty to save.'

Why are your robes all red, O Lord,
and your garments like theirs who tread the winepress?

'I have trodden the winepress alone
and from the peoples no one was with me.'

I will recount the steadfast love of the Lord,
the praises of the Most High.
All that God has done for us in his mercy,
by his many acts of love.

For God said, 'Surely, they are my people,
my children who will not deal falsely,'
and he became their Saviour in all their distress.

So God saved us by his love and pity;
he lifted us up and carried us through all the days of old.

Give praise to the Father . . .

Turn to page 61.

MONDAY

A Song of True Motherhood 3–7 (Julian of Norwich)

Christ came in our poor flesh
to share a mother's care.

Our mothers bear us for pain and for death.
Our true mother, Jesus, bears us for joy and endless life.

Christ carried us within him in love and travail
until the full time of his passion.
And when all was completed and he had carried us so for joy,
still all this could not satisfy the power of his wonderful love.

All that we owe is redeemed in truly loving God,
for the love of Christ works in us.
Christ is the one whom we love.

Give praise to the Father . . .

Turn to page 61.

TUESDAY

A Song of Desertion (Jeremiah 14:17–21)

Let my eyes shed tears day and night,
let them never stop weeping;
for my people have been struck by a crushing blow,
by a very grievous wound.

In the country I see the bodies of those killed by war;
in the city I see people tortured by hunger.
The prophets and priests roam around the country
but they do not know what to do.

Have you completely rejected Judah?
Does your heart loathe Sion?
Why have you struck us down
without hope of a cure?

We were looking for peace, but no good came of it.
We were looking for healing, but we got terror.

Lord, we acknowledge our wickedness and the guilt of our ancestors,
we have indeed sinned against you.
For your name's sake do not reject us or dishonour your glorious throne;
remember us and do not break your covenant with us.

Give praise to the Father . . .

Turn to page 61.

WEDNESDAY

A Song of Lamentation (Lamentations 1:12, 16; 3:19, 22–28, 31–33)

Is it nothing to you, all you who pass by?
Look and see if there is any sorrow like my sorrow,
which was brought upon me,
which the Lord inflicted on the day of his fierce anger.

For these things I weep; my eyes flow with tears,
for a comforter is far from me, one to revive my courage.
Remember my affliction and my bitterness,
the wormwood and the gall!

The steadfast love of the Lord never ceases,
his mercies never come to an end;
they are new every morning,
great is your faithfulness.

'The Lord is my portion,' says my soul,
'therefore I will hope in him.'
The Lord is good to those who wait for him,
to the soul that seeks him.

It is good that we should wait quietly
for the salvation of the Lord.
It is good to bear the yoke in our youth,
to sit alone in silence when it is laid upon us.

For the Lord will not reject for ever.
Though he causes grief, he will have compassion,
according to the abundance of his steadfast love,
for he does not willingly afflict or grieve anyone.

Give praise to the Father . . . **Turn to page 61.**

MAUNDY THURSDAY

A Song of Solomon (Song of Songs 8:6–7)

Set me as a seal upon your heart,
as a seal upon your arm;
for love is strong as death,
passion fierce as the grave.

Its flashes are flashes of fire, a raging flame.
Many waters cannot quench love,
neither can the floods drown it.

If all the wealth of our house were offered for love
it would be utterly scorned.

Give praise to the Father . . . **Turn to page 61.**

GOOD FRIDAY

A Song of Christ the Servant (1 Peter 2:21–25)

> Christ suffered for you,
> leaving you an example
> that you should follow in his steps.
>
> He committed no sin,
> no guile was found on his lips,
> when he was reviled
> he did not revile in turn.
>
> When he suffered, he did not threaten,
> but he trusted in God who judges justly.
>
> Christ himself bore our sins
> in his body on the tree,
> that we might die to sin
> and live to righteousness.
>
> By his wounds you have been healed:
> for you were straying like sheep
> but have now returned
> to the Shepherd and Guardian of your souls.
>
> Give praise to the Father . . .

Turn to page 61.

HOLY SATURDAY

A Song of New Life (Jonah 2:2–9)

> I called to you, O God, out of my distress and you answered me,
> out of the belly of Sheol I cried, and you heard my voice.
> You cast me into the deep, into the heart of the seas,
> and the flood surrounded me, all your waves and billows passed over me.
>
> Then I said, I am driven away from your sight.
> How shall I ever look again upon your holy temple?
>
> The waters closed in over me, the deep was round about me,
> weeds were wrapped around my head at the roots of the mountains.
> I went down to the land beneath the earth,
> yet you brought up my life from the depths, O God.
>
> As my life was ebbing away, I remembered you, O God,
> and my prayer came to you, into your holy temple.
> With the voice of thanksgiving, I will sacrifice to you;
> what I have vowed I will pay, for deliverance belongs to the Lord!
>
> Give praise to the Father . . .

Turn to page 61.

HOLY WEEK – EVERY DAY

The Scripture Reading is read. See Lectionary tables (page 8).

The Responsory (from John 12:32, 27)

V. When I am lifted up from the earth
    I will draw all people to myself.
R. **When I am lifted up from the earth
    I will draw all people to myself.**
V. For this reason I have come to this hour.
R. **I will draw all people to myself.**
V. Glory to the Father, the Son, the Holy Spirit.
R. **When I am lifted up from the earth
    I will draw all people to myself.**

CANTICLE OF THE SEASON

A Song of the Servant (Isaiah 53:3–6)

He was despised, he was rejected,
a man of sorrows, acquainted with grief.
As one from whom people hide their faces
he was despised, and we did not esteem him.

He bore our sufferings,
he endured our torments,
while we thought he was being punished
and struck by God, brought low.

He was pierced for our sins,
bruised for no fault but our own.
His punishment has won our peace,
and by his wounds we are healed.

We have all strayed like sheep
each taking their own way.
But the Lord has laid on him
the guilt of us all.

Give praise to the Father almighty,
to his Son, Jesus Christ, the Lord,
to the Spirit who dwells in our hearts,
both now and for ever. Amen.

PRAYER AND THANKSGIVING

The Lord's Prayer is said. It may be introduced by

As forgiven and forgiving, we pray:
Our Father . . .

Specific intercessions and thanksgivings should be offered here.
This may follow the pattern given in the other seasons of Daily Prayer.

V. We pray to you, Lord Jesus, who suffered for us:
R. **through your death and resurrection, save us.**

V. You laid down your life for your friends:
R. **may we love one another as you have loved us.**

V. You humbled yourself to accept death on the cross:
R. **lead your church into the paschal feast of eternal life.**

V. You made your cross the tree of life:
R. **share your victory with all the baptised.**

V. You died to save us all:
R. **bring into your kingdom all who believe and hope.**

The collect of the day should be said if available.

The following Concluding Prayer is said, or another of your choice:

Christ our victim,
whose beauty was disfigured
and whose body torn upon the cross;
open wide your arms
to embrace our tortured world,
that we may not turn away our eyes,
but abandon ourselves to your mercy. **Amen.**

CONCLUSION

May Christ crucified draw us to himself, to find in him a sure ground for faith, a firm support for hope, and the assurance of sins forgiven. Amen.

DAILY PRAYER

The Season of The Resurrection

Easter Day
until
the Second Sunday of Easter.

After that turn to
The Season of New Life
on page 69.

During Easter Week only the psalms and readings vary, the remainder of *Daily Prayer* being the same every day, emphasising that this is a complete week of Easter Days!

OPENING

V. Alleluia! This is the day the Lord made.

R. **Let us rejoice and be glad. Alleluia!**

Invitatory: The Easter Song of Praise (Exsultet)

Rejoice, heavenly powers! Sing, choirs of angels!
Exult, all creation around God's throne!
Jesus Christ, our King, is risen!
Sound the trumpet of salvation!

Rejoice, O earth, in shining splendour,
radiant in the brightness of your King!
Christ has conquered! Glory fills you!
Darkness vanishes for ever!

Rejoice, O Mother Church! Exult in glory!
The risen Saviour shines upon you!
Let this place resound with joy,
echoing the mighty song of all God's people!

A hymn, or this, or another acclamation may be sung

Alleluia, alleluia,
give thanks to the risen Lord,
Alleluia, alleluia,
give praise to his name.

Opening Prayer

Blessed are you, Lord our God,
you have made this day radiant
by raising your Son Jesus Christ from the dead.

A few words of extempore prayer may be added here

The joy of his resurrection fills our hearts.
May we be witnesses to the world that he is risen,
and lives for ever in your kingdom.

Blessed be God for ever!

The psalm(s) are said. See Lectionary tables (page 8).

Canticle of the Day: The Easter Anthems
(1 Corinthians 5:7–8; Romans 6:9–11; 1 Corinthians 15:20–22)

> Christ our passover has been sacrificed for us
> so let us celebrate the feast:
> not with the old leaven of corruption and wickedness,
> but with the unleavened bread of sincerity and truth.
>
> Christ once raised from the dead dies no more,
> death has no more dominion over him.
> In dying he died to sin once for all,
> in living he lives to God.
>
> See yourselves therefore as dead to sin,
> and alive to God in Jesus Christ our Lord.
>
> Christ has been raised from the dead,
> the first fruits of those who sleep.
>
> For since by one man came death
> by another has come also the resurrection of the dead;
> for as in Adam all die,
> even so in Christ shall all be made alive.

The Scripture Reading is read. See Lectionary tables (page 8).

The Responsory (from Mark 16:6, 15)

> V.   He is not here, he has been raised.
> R.   **He is not here, he has been raised.**
> V.   Tell all the world:
> R.   **he has been raised.**
> V.   Glory to the Father, the Son, the Holy Spirit.
> R.   **He is not here, he has been raised.**

CANTICLE OF THE SEASON

A Song of the Church (Te Deum)

We praise you, O God,
we acclaim you as Lord;
all creation worships you,
the Father everlasting.

To you all angels, all the powers of heaven,
the cherubim and seraphim, sing in endless praise:

Holy, holy, holy Lord,
God of power and might,
heaven and earth are full of your glory.

The glorious company of apostles praise you.
The noble fellowship of prophets praise you.

The white-robed army of martyrs praise you.
Throughout the world the holy Church acclaims you:

Father, of majesty unbounded,
your true and only Son, worthy of all praise,
the Holy Spirit, advocate and guide.

You, Christ, are the king of glory,
the eternal Son of the Father.

When you took our flesh to set us free
you humbly chose the Virgin's womb.
You overcame the sting of death
and opened the kingdom of heaven to all believers.

You are seated at God's right hand in glory.
We believe that you will come to be our judge.

Come then, Lord, and help your people,
bought with the price of your own blood,
and bring us with your saints to glory everlasting.

PRAYER AND THANKSGIVING

The Lord's Prayer is said. It may be introduced by
Delivered and made new in Christ, we pray:
Our Father . . .

Specific intercessions and thanksgivings should be offered here.
This may follow the pattern given in the other seasons of Daily Prayer.

V.   We pray to you, Lord Christ; you have been raised for us:
R.   **you reign with the Father and intercede for us.**

V.   You are the light of the world and the salvation of the nations:
R.   **empower us to proclaim the wonder of your resurrection.**

V.   Let all the world recognise you as the Messiah:
R.   **fill everyone with the knowledge of your glory.**

V.   You have overcome death, the last enemy of humanity:
R.   **destroy everything in us that is at enmity with God.**

V.   You were obedient even unto death, but God raised you to glory:
R.   **receive us all into your glorious kingdom.**

The collect of the day should be said if available.

The following Concluding Prayer is said, or another of your choice:
Christ, you are risen from the dead.
We are risen with you.
May our life never deny
this eternal life,
this peace and hope and joy.
Praise and glory to the God of life
who is stronger than all kinds of death. **Alleluia.**

CONCLUSION

**Christ is risen indeed from the dead. Glory and power are
his for ever and ever. Alleluia!**

DAILY PRAYER

The Season of New Life

Monday of the Second Week of Eastertide
until
Pentecost inclusive.

After that turn to
Through the Year
on page 8 1,
resuming in *The Lectionary*
on whatever date it is.

OPENING

V. The Lord is risen. Alleluia!

R. **Come, let us worship.**

Invitatory: Psalm 118:1, 15, 19–20, 22–23

Give thanks to the Lord who is good,
for God's love endures for ever.
There are shouts of joy and victory
in the tents of the just.

Open to me the gates of holiness:
I will enter and give thanks.
This is the Lord's own gate
where the just may enter.

The stone which the builders rejected
has become the cornerstone.
This is the work of the Lord,
a marvel in our eyes.

Give praise to the Father almighty,
to his Son, Jesus Christ, the Lord,
to the Spirit who dwells in our hearts,
both now and for ever. Amen.

Alleluia!

A hymn, or this, or another acclamation may be sung

He is Lord, he is Lord.
He is risen from the dead and he is Lord.
Ev'ry knee shall bow, ev'ry tongue confess
that Jesus Christ is Lord.

Opening Prayer

Blessed and praised are you, God our Father,
for raising Christ our Lord from the dead
and giving us the hope of immortality.

A few words of extempore prayer may be added here

The joy of the resurrection renews the whole world:
a new age has dawned,
the reign of sin is ended,
a broken world is being renewed,
and humanity is once again made whole.

Blessed be God for ever!

Daily Prayer continues on the following pages according to the day.

SUNDAY

The psalm(s) are said. See Lectionary tables (pages 8–9).

Canticle of the Day: The Easter Anthems
(1) Corinthians 5:7–8; Romans 6:9–11; 1 Corinthians 15:20–22)

> Christ our passover has been sacrificed for us
> so let us celebrate the feast:
> not with the old leaven of corruption and wickedness,
> but with the unleavened bread of sincerity and truth.
>
> Christ once raised from the dead dies no more,
> death has no more dominion over him.
> In dying he died to sin once for all,
> in living he lives to God.
>
> See yourselves therefore as dead to sin,
> and alive to God in Jesus Christ our Lord.
>
> Christ has been raised from the dead,
> the first fruits of those who sleep.
>
> For since by one man came death
> by another has come also the resurrection of the dead;
> for as in Adam all die,
> even so in Christ shall all be made alive.

The Scripture Reading is read. See Lectionary tables (pages 8–9).

The Responsory (from 1 Peter 2:9)
> V. You are called into God's marvellous light.
> R. **You are called into God's marvellous light.**
> V. A chosen race, a royal priesthood,
> R. **called into God's marvellous light.**
> V. Glory to the Father, the Son, the Holy Spirit.
> R. **You are called into God's marvellous light.**

Daily Prayer continues with the Canticle of the Season on page 78.

MONDAY

The psalm(s) are said. See Lectionary tables (pages 8–9).

Canticle of the Day: A Song of Deliverance (Isaiah 12:2–6)

> Behold, God is my salvation,
> I will trust and will not be afraid;
> for the Lord God is my strength and my song
> and has become my salvation.
>
> With joy you will draw water
> from the wells of salvation.
>
> On that day you will say:
> Give thanks to the Lord, call upon his name;
> make known his deeds among the nations,
> proclaim that his name is exalted.
>
> Sing God's praises, who has triumphed gloriously,
> let this be known in all the world.
> Shout and sing for joy, you that dwell in Zion,
> for great in your midst is the Holy One of Israel.
>
> Give praise to the Father . . .

The Scripture Reading is read. See Lectionary tables (pages 8–9).

The Responsory (from 1 Peter 2:5)

V. Like living stones, be built into a spiritual house.
R. **Like living stones, be built into a spiritual house.**
V. Offer sacrifices acceptable to God.
R. **Be built into a spiritual house.**
V. Glory to the Father, the Son, the Holy Spirit.
R. **Like living stones, be built into a spiritual house.**

Daily Prayer continues with the Canticle of the Season on page 78.

TUESDAY

The psalm(s) are said. See Lectionary tables (pages 8–9).

Canticle of the Day: A Song of Faith (1 Peter 1:3–4, 18–21)

Blessed be the God
and Father of our Lord Jesus Christ,
who in his great mercy
gave us a new birth as his children.

He has raised Jesus Christ from the dead
so that we have a sure hope in him.
We have the promise of an inheritance
that can never be spoilt
because it is kept for us in heaven.

The ransom that was paid to free us
was not paid in silver or gold,
but in the precious blood of Christ,
the Lamb without spot or stain.

God raised him from the dead and gave him glory,
so that we might have faith and hope in God.

Give praise to the Father . . .

The Scripture Reading is read. See Lectionary tables (pages 8–9).

The Responsory (from 1 Peter 1:15)

V.   As he who called you is holy, be holy yourselves.
R.   **As he who called you is holy, be holy yourselves.**
V.   You shall be holy, for I am holy.
R.   **Be holy yourselves.**
V.   Glory to the Father, the Son, the Holy Spirit.
R.   **As he who called you is holy, be holy yourselves.**

Daily Prayer continues with the Canticle of the Season on page 78.

WEDNESDAY

The psalm(s) are said. See Lectionary tables (pages 8–9).

Canticle of the Day: A Song of the Bride (Isaiah 61:10–62:3)

> I will greatly rejoice in the Lord,
> my soul shall exult in my God;
> who has clothed me with the garments of salvation
> and has covered me with the cloak of integrity,
> as a bridegroom decks himself with a garland
> and as a bride adorns herself with her jewels.
>
> For as the earth puts forth her blossom,
> and as seeds in the garden spring up,
> so shall God make righteousness and praise
> blossom before all the nations.
>
> For Zion's sake, I will not keep silent,
> and for Jerusalem's sake, I will not rest,
> until her deliverance shines out like the dawn
> and her salvation as a burning torch.
>
> The nations shall see your deliverance
> and all rulers shall see your glory;
> then you shall be called by a new name
> which the mouth of God will give.
>
> You shall be a crown of glory
> in the hand of the Lord,
> a royal diadem in the hand of your God.
>
> Give praise to the Father . . .

The Scripture Reading is read. See Lectionary tables (pages 8–9).

The Responsory (from 1 Peter 1:23)

V.   You have been born anew, through the living word of God.
R.   **You have been born anew, through the living word of God.**
V.   Not of perishable, but of imperishable seed:
R.   **through the living word of God.**
V.   Glory to the Father, the Son, the Holy Spirit.
R.   **You have been born anew, through the living word of God.**

Daily Prayer continues with the Canticle of the Season on page 78.

THURSDAY

The psalm(s) are said. See Lectionary tables (pages 8–9).

Canticle of the Day: A Song of God's Grace (Ephesians 1:3–10)

>Blessed are you, the God and Father
>of our Lord Jesus Christ,
>for you have blest us in Christ Jesus
>with every spiritual blessing in the heavenly places.
>
>You chose us to be yours in Christ
>before the foundation of the world,
>that we should be holy and blameless before you.
>
>In love you destined us to be your children,
>through Jesus Christ, according to the purpose of your will,
>to the praise of your glorious grace
>which you freely bestowed on us in the Beloved.
>
>In you, we have redemption through the blood of Christ –
>the forgiveness of our sins,
>according to the riches of your grace
>which you have lavished upon us.
>
>You have made known to us
>in all wisdom and insight
>the mystery of your will;
>according to your purpose
>which you set forth in Christ
>as a plan for the fullness of time,
>
>to unite all things in Christ,
>things in heaven and things on earth.
>
>Give praise to the Father . . .

The Scripture Reading is read. See Lectionary tables (pages 8–9).

The Responsory (from 1 Peter 1:8)

>V.   Although you have not seen him, you love him.
>R.   **Although you have not seen him, you love him.**
>V.   You believe in him and rejoice.
>R.   **You love him.**
>V.   Glory to the Father, the Son, the Holy Spirit.
>R.   **Although you have not seen him, you love him.**

Daily Prayer continues with the Canticle of the Season on page 78.

FRIDAY

The psalm(s) are said. See Lectionary tables (pages 8–9).

Canticle of the Day: The Song of Mary (Luke 1:46–55)

My soul proclaims the greatness of the Lord,
my spirit rejoices in God my Saviour,
who has looked with favour on his lowly servant.

From this day all generations will call me blessed:
the Almighty has done great things for me
and holy is his name.
God has mercy on those who fear him,
from generation to generation.

The Lord has shown strength with his arm
and scattered the proud in their conceit,
casting down the mighty from their thrones
and lifting up the lowly.

God has filled the hungry with good things
and sent the rich away empty.

He has come to the aid of his servant Israel,
to remember the promise of mercy,
the promise made to our forebears,
to Abraham and his children for ever.

Give praise to the Father . . .

The Scripture Reading is read. See Lectionary tables (pages 8–9).

The Responsory (from 1 Peter 1:21)

V.   You have come to trust in God, who raised Christ from the dead.
R.   **You have come to trust in God, who raised Christ from the dead.**
V.   Your faith and hope are set on God,
R.   **who raised Christ from the dead.**
V.   Glory to the Father, the Son, the Holy Spirit.
R.   **You have come to trust in God, who raised Christ from the dead.**

Daily Prayer continues with the Canticle of the Season on page 78.

SATURDAY

The psalm(s) are said. See Lectionary tables (pages 8–9).

Canticle of the Day: The Song of Moses and Miriam
(Exodus 15:1b–2, 6a, 8, 13–18)

I will sing to the Lord, who has triumphed gloriously,
the horse and his rider have been thrown into the sea.

The Lord is my strength and my song
and has become my salvation.
This is my God whom I will praise,
the God of my forebears whom I will exalt.

The Lord fights for his people,
the Lord is his name.

Your right hand, O Lord,
is glorious in power.
Your right hand, O Lord,
shatters the enemy.

At the blast of your nostrils
the sea covered them.
They sank as lead in the mighty waters.

In your unfailing love, O Lord,
you lead the people whom you have redeemed,
and by your invincible strength
you will guide them to your holy dwelling.

You will bring them in and plant them, O Lord,
in the sanctuary which your hands have established.

Give praise to the Father . . .

The Scripture Reading is read. See Lectionary tables (pages 8–9).

The Responsory (from 1 Peter 1:4)
  V.   God has given us an everlasting inheritance.
  R.   **God has given us an everlasting inheritance.**
  V.   Undefiled and unfading, kept in heaven for you;
  R.   **an everlasting inheritance.**
  V.   Glory to the Father, the Son, the Holy Spirit.
  R.   **God has given us an everlasting inheritance.**

Daily Prayer continues with the Canticle of the Season on page 78.

EVERY DAY

CANTICLE OF THE SEASON

A Song of the Church (Te Deum)

We praise you, O God,
we acclaim you as Lord;
all creation worships you,
the Father everlasting.

To you all angels, all the powers of heaven,
the cherubim and seraphim, sing in endless praise:

Holy, holy, holy Lord,
God of power and might,
heaven and earth are full of your glory.

The glorious company of apostles praise you.
The noble fellowship of prophets praise you.

The white-robed army of martyrs praise you.
Throughout the world the holy Church acclaims you:

Father, of majesty unbounded,
your true and only Son, worthy of all praise,
the Holy Spirit, advocate and guide.

You, Christ, are the king of glory,
the eternal Son of the Father.

When you took our flesh to set us free
you humbly chose the Virgin's womb.
You overcame the sting of death
and opened the kingdom of heaven to all believers.

You are seated at God's right hand in glory.
We believe that you will come to be our judge.

Come then, Lord, and help your people,
bought with the price of your own blood,
and bring us with your saints to glory everlasting.

PRAYER AND THANKSGIVING

The Lord's Prayer is said. It may be introduced by
>Delivered and made new in Christ, we pray:
>Our Father . . .

Specific intercessions and thanksgivings should be offered here.
These may begin with:

Today	its encounters, opportunities and demands.
Currently	concerns and achievements in our churches and society: locally, nationally and around the world.

A personal Prayer Diary or some other Cycle of Intercession may guide further prayer.

Prayer may also be offered using one or more of the following categories:

Local	Community life, work, leisure, education. The sick, the bereaved, the lonely. The witness and fellowship of God's people.
National	Government, commerce and industry, institutions. The unemployed, victims of crime, or marginalised. The Church: its leaders and its prophetic role.
Global	Nations and their leaders; justice, peace and development. Refugees and victims of war. The dispossessed, the hungry, the persecuted. The Church: its partnership in world mission.

The period of prayer is concluded with the following responses:
V. Give thanks to the Lord, for he is gracious:
R. **he has loved us from all eternity.**

V. By his cross and resurrection he has redeemed the world:
R. **and has washed us from our sins in his blood.**

V. On the third day he rose again:
R. **and has given us the victory.**

V. He ascended into heaven:
R. **and opened for us the gate to everlasting life.**

V. He is seated at the right hand of the Father:
R. **and lives for ever to intercede for us.**

The collect of the day should be said if available.

One or more of these Concluding Prayers is said, or another of your choice:

Living God,
for whom no door is closed,
no heart is locked,
draw us beyond our doubts,
till we see your Christ
and touch his wounds
where they bleed in others. **Amen.**

Hail, O beauty of the Father!
Hail, O power of the Son!
Hail, O Spirit most pure,
    bond of the Father and the Son!
O Christ, send down on us
    this Spirit with the Father,
    that he may sprinkle our souls with his dew
    and fill them with his royal gifts. **Amen.**

Spirit of the living Christ,
    come upon us in the glory of your risen power;
Spirit of the living Christ,
    come upon us in all the humility of your wondrous love;
Spirit of the living Christ,
    come upon us that new life may course within our veins,
    new love bind us together in one family,
    a new vision of the kingdom of God spur us on
    to serve you with fearless passion. **Amen.**

Christ our life, you are alive!
You set before us a great choice,
    therefore we choose life.
The dance of the resurrection soars and surges
    through the whole creation.
It sets gifts of bread and wine upon our table.
    This is grace, dying we live.
    So let us live. **Amen.**

CONCLUSION

**May Christ, who out of defeat has brought us hope, fill us with new life.
Amen**

DAILY PRAYER

Through the Year

3 February
until
Shrove Tuesday.

Also from
the Monday following Pentecost
until 31 October.

After Shrove Tuesday turn to *The Season of Penitence*
on page 43.

After 31 October turn to *The Season of Joyful Hope*
on page 19.

In this season only, the Lectionary follows a three-year cycle as in the Revised Common Lectionary which is used by many churches. In 2002 we use the readings for Year A, with future years following the table below:

Year A	2002	2005	2008	2011	2014	2017	etc.
Year B	2003	2006	2009	2012	2015	2018	etc.
Year C	2004	2007	2010	2013	2016	2019	etc.

OPENING

V. The Lord is our light and our life:

R. **Come, let us worship.**

Invitatory: Psalm 100

Cry out with joy to the Lord, all the earth.
Serve the Lord with gladness.
Come before God, singing for joy.

Know that the Lord is God,
our maker, to whom we belong.
We are God's people, sheep of the flock.

Enter the gates with thanksgiving,
God's courts with songs of praise.
Give thanks to God and bless his name.

Indeed, how good is the Lord,
whose merciful love is eternal;
whose faithfulness lasts forever.

Give praise to the Father almighty,
to his Son, Jesus Christ, the Lord,
to the Spirit who dwells in our hearts,
both now and for ever. Amen.

Alleluia!

A hymn, or either of these, or another acclamation may be sung

Bless the Lord, my soul,	*or*	The Lord is my light,
and bless God's holy name.		my light and salvation:
Bless the Lord, my soul,		in God I trust,
who leads me into life.		in God I trust.

Opening Prayer

Blessed are you, O Lord our God,
you are our life and salvation;
yours is the glory, this day and always.

A few words of extempore prayer may be added here

Open our eyes to behold your presence
and strengthen our hands in doing your will;
that the world may rejoice and give you praise,
Father, Son, and Holy Spirit.

Blessed be God for ever!

Daily Prayer continues on the following pages according to the day.

SUNDAY

The psalm(s) are said. See Lectionary tables (pages 5–6, 10–14).

Canticle of the Day: The Song of Zechariah (Luke 1:68–79)

Blessed be the Lord, the God of Israel,
who has come to his people and set them free.
The Lord has raised up for us a mighty Saviour,
born of the house of his servant David.

Through the holy prophets, God promised of old
to save us from our enemies,
from the hands of all who hate us,
to show mercy to our forebears,
and to remember his holy covenant.

This was the oath God swore to our father Abraham:
to set us free from the hands of our enemies,
free to worship him without fear,
holy and righteous before him,
all the days of our life.

And you, child, shall be called the prophet of the Most High,
for you will go before the Lord to prepare his way,
to give his people knowledge of salvation
by the forgiveness of their sins.

In the tender compassion of our God
the dawn from on high shall break upon us,
to shine on those who dwell in darkness and the shadow of death,
and to guide our feet into the way of peace.

Give praise to the Father . . .

The Scripture Reading is read. See Lectionary tables (pages 5–6, 10–14).

The Responsory (from Psalm 119:169, 173)

V.   I rejoice before you, Lord, let your word bring me light.
R.   **I rejoice before you, Lord, let your word bring me light.**
V.   Reach out and lead me,
R.   **let your word bring me light.**
V.   Glory to the Father, the Son, the Holy Spirit.
R.   **I rejoice before you, Lord, let your word bring me light.**

Daily Prayer continues with the Canticle of the Season on page 90.

MONDAY

The psalm(s) are said. See Lectionary tables (pages 5–6, 10–14).

Canticle of the Day: A Song of Praise (Revelation 4:11; 5:9b–10, 13)

You are worthy
our Lord and God,
to receive glory
and honour and power;

for you have created all things
and by your will they have their being.

You are worthy
O Lamb, for you were slain;
and by your blood you ransomed for God
saints from every tribe and language and nation.

You have made them to be a kingdom
and priests serving our God,
and they will reign with you on earth.

To the One who sits on the throne
and to the Lamb
be blessing and honour and glory and might,
for ever and ever. Amen.

The Scripture Reading is read. See Lectionary tables (pages 5–6, 10–14).

The Responsory (from Psalm 119:14, 16)

   V.   I treasure your ways more than great riches.
   R.   **I treasure your ways more than great riches.**
   V.   I delight in your rules,
   R.   **more than great riches.**
   V.   Glory to the Father, the Son, the Holy Spirit.
   R.   **I treasure your ways more than great riches.**

Daily Prayer continues with the Canticle of the Season on page 90.

TUESDAY

The psalm(s) are said. See Lectionary tables (pages 5–6, 10–14).

Canticle of the Day: A Song of Creation (from Song of the Three 35–65)

Bless the Lord all created things,
he is worthy to be praised and exalted for ever.
Bless the Lord you heavens,
he is worthy to be praised and exalted for ever.

O let the earth bless the Lord; bless the Lord you mountains and hills,
bless the Lord all that grows in the ground,
he is worthy to be praised and exalted for ever.

Bless the Lord you springs, bless the Lord you seas and rivers,
bless the Lord you whales and all that swim in the waters,
he is worthy to be praised and exalted for ever.

Bless the Lord all birds of the air, bless the Lord you beasts and cattle,
bless the Lord all people of the earth,
he is worthy to be praised and exalted for ever.

O People of God bless the Lord; bless the Lord you priests of the Lord,
bless the Lord you servants of the Lord,
he is worthy to be praised and exalted for ever.

Bless the Lord all you of upright spirit,
bless the Lord you that are holy and humble in heart,
bless the Father, the Son, the Holy Spirit:
God, who is worthy to be praised and exalted for ever. Amen.

The Scripture Reading is read. See Lectionary tables (pages 5–6, 10–14).

The Responsory (from Psalm 119:64, 58)

V. Lord, your love fills the earth; teach me your laws.
R. **Lord, your love fills the earth; teach me your laws.**
V. I pray from my heart,
R. **teach me your laws.**
V. Glory to the Father, the Son, the Holy Spirit.
R. **Lord, your love fills the earth; teach me your laws.**

Daily Prayer continues with the Canticle of the Season on page 90.

WEDNESDAY

The psalm(s) are said. See Lectionary tables (pages 5–6, 10–14).

Canticle of the Day: The Song of Mary (Luke 1:46–55)

>My soul proclaims the greatness of the Lord,
>my spirit rejoices in God my Saviour,
>who has looked with favour on his lowly servant.
>
>From this day all generations will call me blessed:
>the Almighty has done great things for me
>and holy is his name.
>God has mercy on those who fear him,
>from generation to generation.
>
>The Lord has shown strength with his arm
>and scattered the proud in their conceit,
>casting down the mighty from their thrones
>and lifting up the lowly.
>
>God has filled the hungry with good things
>and sent the rich away empty.
>
>He has come to the aid of his servant Israel,
>to remember the promise of mercy,
>the promise made to our forebears,
>to Abraham and his children for ever.
>
>Give praise to the Father . . .

The Scripture Reading is read. See Lectionary tables (pages 5–6, 10–14).

The Responsory (from Psalm 119:105, 111)

V.   Your word is a lamp for my steps, a light for my path.
R.   **Your word is a lamp for my steps, a light for my path.**
V.   Your laws are my heritage;
R.   **a light for my path.**
V.   Glory to the Father, the Son, the Holy Spirit.
R.   **Your word is a lamp for my steps, a light for my path.**

Daily Prayer continues with the Canticle of the Season on page 90.

THURSDAY

The psalm(s) are said. See Lectionary tables (pages 5–6, 10–14).

Canticle of the Day: A Song of God's Reign (Tobit 13:1–6)

> Blessed be God, who lives for ever,
> whose reign endures throughout all ages.
>
> Declare God's praise before the nations,
> you who are the children of Israel.
> For if our God has scattered you among them,
> there too has he shown you his greatness.
>
> Exalt him in the sight of the living,
> because he is our God and our Father for ever.
>
> Though God punishes you for your wickedness,
> mercy will be shown to you all.
> God will gather you from every nation,
> from wherever you have been scattered.
>
> See what the Lord has done for you
> and give thanks with a loud voice.
> Praise the Lord of righteousness
> and exalt the King of the ages.
>
> Give praise to the Father . . .

The Scripture Reading is read. See Lectionary tables (pages 5–6, 10–14).

The Responsory (from Psalm 119:89, 90)

V. Your word is for ever, Lord, fixed in the heavens.
R. **Your word is for ever, Lord, fixed in the heavens.**
V. Your faithfulness is eternal,
R. **fixed in the heavens.**
V. Glory to the Father, the Son, the Holy Spirit.
R. **Your word is for ever, Lord, fixed in the heavens.**

Daily Prayer continues with the Canticle of the Season on page 90.

FRIDAY

The psalm(s) are said. See Lectionary tables (pages 5–6, 10–14).

Canticle of the Day: A Song of Christ's Goodness (Anselm)

>Jesus, as a mother you gather your people to you;
>you are gentle with us as a mother with her children.
>
>Often you weep over our sins and our pride,
>tenderly you draw us from hatred and judgement.
>You comfort us in sorrow and bind up our wounds,
>in sickness you nurse us and with pure milk you feed us.
>
>Jesus, by your dying, we are born to new life;
>by your anguish and labour we come forth in joy.
>
>Despair turns to hope through your sweet goodness;
>through your gentleness, we find comfort in fear.
>Your warmth gives life to the dead,
>your touch makes sinners righteous.
>
>Lord Jesus, in your mercy, heal us;
>in your love and tenderness, remake us,
>in your compassion, bring grace and forgiveness,
>for the beauty of heaven, may your love prepare us.
>
>Give praise to the Father . . .

The Scripture Reading is read. See Lectionary tables (pages 5–6, 10–14).

The Responsory (from Psalm 119:124, 125)

>V.   God, be merciful, show me your ways.
>R.   **God, be merciful, show me your ways.**
>V.   Help me understand,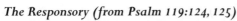
>R.   **show me your ways.**
>V.   Glory to the Father, the Son, the Holy Spirit.
>R.   **God, be merciful, show me your ways.**

Daily Prayer continues with the Canticle of the Season on page 90.

SATURDAY

The psalm(s) are said. See Lectionary tables (pages 5–6, 10–14).

Canticle of the Day: A Song of the Blessed (Matthew 5:3–12)

> Blessed are the poor in spirit,
> for theirs is the kingdom of heaven.
>
> Blessed are those who mourn,
> for they shall be comforted.
>
> Blessed are the gentle,
> for they shall inherit the earth.
>
> Blessed are those who hunger and thirst for what is right,
> for they shall be satisfied.
>
> Blessed are the merciful,
> for mercy shall be shown to them.
>
> Blessed are the pure in heart,
> for they shall see God.
>
> Blessed are the peacemakers,
> for they shall be called the children of God.
>
> Blessed are those who are persecuted in the cause of right,
> for theirs is the kingdom of heaven.
>
> Blessed are you when others revile you and persecute you
> and utter all kinds of evil against you falsely for my sake.
>
> Rejoice and be glad
> for your reward is great in heaven.

The Scripture Reading is read. See Lectionary tables (pages 5–6, 10–14).

The Responsory (from Psalm 119:131, 130)

> V. Longing for you, I thirst for your teaching.
> R. **Longing for you, I thirst for your teaching.**
> V. Unfold your word,
> R. **I thirst for your teaching.**
> V. Glory to the Father, the Son, the Holy Spirit.
> R. **Longing for you, I thirst for your teaching.**

Daily Prayer continues with the Canticle of the Season on page 90.

EVERY DAY

CANTICLE OF THE SEASON

Either: The Song of Christ's Glory (Philippians 2:5b–11)

Christ Jesus was in the form of God,
but he did not cling to equality with God.

He emptied himself,
taking the form of a servant,
and was born in our human likeness.

Being found in human form he humbled himself
and became obedient unto death, even death on a cross;

therefore, God has highly exalted him,
and bestowed on him the name above every name,

that at the name of Jesus every knee shall bow,
in heaven and on earth and under the earth;

and every tongue confess that Jesus Christ is Lord,
to the glory of God the Father.

Give praise to the Father almighty,
to his Son, Jesus Christ, the Lord,
to the Spirit who dwells in our hearts,
both now and for ever. Amen.

Or: A Song of Faith (1 Peter 1:3–4, 18–21)

Blessed be the God
and Father of our Lord Jesus Christ,
who in his great mercy
gave us a new birth as his children.

He has raised Jesus Christ from the dead
so that we have a sure hope in him.
We have the promise of an inheritance
that can never be spoilt
because it is kept for us in heaven.

The ransom that was paid to free us
was not paid in silver or gold,
but in the precious blood of Christ,
the Lamb without spot or stain.

God raised him from the dead and gave him glory,
so that we might have faith and hope in God.

Give praise to the Father almighty,
to his Son, Jesus Christ, the Lord,
to the Spirit who dwells in our hearts,
both now and for ever. Amen.

PRAYER AND THANKSGIVING

The Lord's Prayer is said. It may be introduced by

As Jesus taught us, we pray:
Our Father...

Specific intercessions and thanksgivings should be offered here.
These may begin with:

Today   its encounters, opportunities and demands.
Currently   concerns and achievements in our churches and society:
            locally, nationally and around the world.

A personal Prayer Diary or some other Cycle of Intercession may guide further prayer.

Prayer may also be offered using one or more of the following categories:

Local   Community life, work, leisure, education.
           The sick, the bereaved, the lonely.
           The witness and fellowship of God's people.
National   Government, commerce and industry, institutions.
           The unemployed, victims of crime, or marginalised.
           The Church: its leaders and its prophetic role.
Global   Nations and their leaders; justice, peace and development.
           Refugees and victims of war.
           The dispossessed, the hungry, the persecuted.
           The Church: its partnership in world mission.

The period of prayer is concluded with the following responses:

V. Make your ways known upon the earth, Lord God:
R. **your saving power among all peoples.**

V. Renew your Church in holiness:
R. **and help us to serve you with joy.**

V. Guide the leaders of this and every nation:
R. **that justice may prevail throughout the world.**

V. Do not let the needy be forgotten:
R. **nor the hope of the poor be taken away.**

V. Make us instruments of your peace:
R. **and let your glory be over all the earth.**

The collect of the day should be said if available.

One or more of these Concluding Prayers is said, or another of your choice:

Holy and eternal God,
give us such trust in your sure purpose,
    that we measure our lives
    not by what we have done or failed to do,
    but by our faithfulness to you. **Amen.**

Almighty God,
    you have made us for yourself,
    and our hearts are restless
    until they find their rest in you.
Grant us purity of heart and strength of purpose
    that in your service we may find our perfect freedom;
    through Jesus Christ our Lord. **Amen.**

Be a bright flame before me,
be a guiding star above me,
be a smooth path below me,
be a kindly shepherd behind me,
this day and for ever. **Amen.**

Fill us, Father,
    with your Spirit of joy and hope
and guide us on our pilgrimage of faith;
that we may walk with him
who is the way, the truth, and the life;
your Son, our Saviour Jesus Christ. **Amen.**

CONCLUSION

The grace of our Lord Jesus Christ, and the love of God, and the fellowship of the Holy Spirit be with us all evermore. Amen.

DAILY PRAYER

Saints' and Holy Days

For use on Saints' Days and other Holy Days

This section follows the same format as the seasonal orders of *Daily Prayer* except that instead of material varying with the day of the week it varies with the category of festival being celebrated. Thus there are two Opening pages, depending on whether the festival is a Holy Day (L) or a Saint's Day; and then instead of turning to the page for Tuesday or Thursday, for example, for the Canticle of the Day and Responsory, you would turn to the page for Apostles and Evangelists (AE) for St Mark, or Martyrs (M) for St Stephen.

Principal Saints' Days and Festivals are given proper psalms and Scripture readings in the Lectionary tables on the appropriate calendar date.

Other Saints' days can easily be kept by using the supplementary table on page 18, which also contains festivals that are not specific to a calendar date. Decide which of the categories best suits the saint to be celebrated and use one of the sets of psalms and readings given in that table.

OPENING – HOLY DAYS (L)

V.   Holy, holy, holy is the Lord God almighty:
R.   **Come, let us worship.**

Invitatory: Psalm 24:1–2, 9–10

The Lord's is the earth and its fullness,
the world and all its peoples.
It is God who set it on the seas;
who made it firm on the waters.

O gates, lift high your heads;
grow higher, ancient doors.
Let the king of glory enter!

Who is the king of glory?
The Lord of heavenly armies.
This is the king of glory.

Give praise to the Father almighty,
to his Son, Jesus Christ, the Lord,
to the Spirit who dwells in our hearts,
both now and for ever. Amen.

Alleluia! *(omitted in Lent)*

A hymn, or this, or another acclamation may be sung

Father, we adore you,
lay our lives before you.
How we love you!

Jesus, we adore you . . .

Spirit, we adore you . . .

Opening Prayer

Blessed are you, O Lord our God,
you have shone in our hearts
to give the light of the knowledge of your glory
in the face of Jesus Christ.

A few words of extempore prayer may be added here

May Christ's life be made visible in us
as we honour him as Lord.

Blessed be God for ever!

Daily Prayer continues on page 96.

OPENING – SAINTS' DAYS

V. The Lord is glorious in his Saints:
R. **Come, let us worship.**

Invitatory: Psalm 24:3–6

Who shall climb the mountain of the Lord?
Who shall stand in God's holy place?
Those with clean hands and pure hearts,
who desire not worthless things,
who have not sworn so as to deceive their neighbour.

They shall receive blessings from the Lord
and reward from the God who saves them.
These are the ones who seek,
seek the face of the God of Jacob.

Give praise to the Father almighty,
to his Son, Jesus Christ, the Lord,
to the Spirit who dwells in our hearts,
both now and for ever. Amen.

Alleluia! (*omitted in Lent*)

A hymn, or this, or another acclamation may be sung

Abba, Father, let me be
yours and yours alone.
May my will for ever be
more and more your own.
Never let my heart grow cold,
never let me go.
Abba, Father, let me be
yours and yours alone.

Opening Prayer

God of glory,
you have given us a great cloud of witnesses
who inspire us on our pilgrimage of faith.

A few words of extempore prayer may be added here

Accept our offering of praise and worship
as we celebrate this feast of *Saint N.*
that we may live our lives in faithfulness and love.

Blessed be God for ever!

Daily Prayer continues on pages 97–101 according to the category of the saint.

HOLY DAYS (L)

The psalm(s) are said. See Lectionary tables (pages 4–18).

Canticle of the Day:
A Song of the Lamb (Revelation 19:1b, 5b, 6b–7, 9b)

> Salvation and glory and power
> belong to our God
> whose judgements are true and just.

> Praise our God
> all you servants of God,
> you who fear him,
> both small and great.

> The Lord our God
> the Almighty reigns;
> let us rejoice and exult
> and give glory and homage.

> The marriage of the Lamb has come
> and his bride has made herself ready;
> happy are those who are invited
> to the wedding banquet of the Lamb.

> To the One who sits on the throne,
> and to the Lamb,
> be blessing and honour
> and glory and might,
> for ever and ever. Amen.

The Scripture Reading is read. See Lectionary tables (pages 4–18).

The Responsory (from Psalm 96:2–3)

V.   Proclaim the glory of the Lord to all the nations.
R.   **Proclaim the glory of the Lord to all the nations.**
V.   Announce it to all his people,
R.   **to all the nations.**
V.   Glory to the Father, the Son, the Holy Spirit.
R.   **Proclaim the glory of the Lord to all the nations.**

Daily Prayer continues with the Canticle of the Season on page 102.

APOSTLES AND EVANGELISTS (AE)

The psalm(s) are said. See Lectionary tables (pages 4–18).

Canticle of the Day:
A Song of God's Assembled (Hebrews 12:22–24, 28–29)

> We have come before God's holy mountain,
> to the heavenly Jerusalem,
> the city of the living God.
>
> We have come before countless angels making festival,
> before the assembly of the first-born citizens of heaven.
>
> We have come before God,
> the righteous judge of all,
> before the spirits of the just made perfect.
>
> We are come before Jesus,
> the mediator of the new covenant;
> we are receiving a kingdom that cannot be shaken,
> let us therefore give thanks to our God,
>
> and offer God an acceptable worship
> full of reverence and awe,
> for our God is a consuming fire.
>
> Give praise to the Father . . .

The Scripture Reading is read. See Lectionary tables (pages 4–18).

The Responsory (from Revelation 7:9)

> V.   They stand before the throne and the Lamb.
> R.   **They stand before the throne and the Lamb.**
> V.   Dressed in white robes with palms in their hands,
> R.   **before the throne and the Lamb.**
> V.   Glory to the Father, the Son, the Holy Spirit.
> R.   **They stand before the throne and the Lamb.**

Daily Prayer continues with the Canticle of the Season on page 102.

THE VIRGIN MARY (VM)

The psalm(s) are said. See Lectionary tables (pages 4–18).

Canticle of the Day: The Song of Mary (Luke 1:46–55)

    My soul proclaims the greatness of the Lord,
    my spirit rejoices in God my Saviour,
    who has looked with favour on his lowly servant.

    From this day all generations will call me blessed:
    the Almighty has done great things for me
    and holy is his name.
    God has mercy on those who fear him,
    from generation to generation.

    The Lord has shown strength with his arm
    and scattered the proud in their conceit,
    casting down the mighty from their thrones
    and lifting up the lowly.

    God has filled the hungry with good things
    and sent the rich away empty.

    He has come to the aid of his servant Israel,
    to remember the promise of mercy,
    the promise made to our forebears,
    to Abraham and his children for ever.

    Give praise to the Father . . .

The Scripture Reading is read. See Lectionary tables (pages 4–18).

The Responsory (from Luke 1:28, 42)

    V.   Hail Mary, full of grace, the Lord is with you.
    R.   **Hail Mary, full of grace, the Lord is with you.**
    V.   Blessed are you among women,
    R.   **the Lord is with you.**
    V.   Glory to the Father, the Son, the Holy Spirit.
    R.   **Hail Mary, full of grace, the Lord is with you.**

Daily Prayer continues with the Canticle of the Season on page 102.

MARTYRS (M)

The psalm(s) are said. See Lectionary tables (pages 4–18).

Canticle of the Day: A Song of the Righteous (Wisdom 3:1–8)

The souls of the righteous
are in the hand of God,
and no torment will ever touch them.

In the eyes of the foolish
they seem to have died,
but they are at peace.

For though,
in the sight of others
they were punished,
their hope is of immortality.

Having been disciplined a little
they will receive great good,
because God tested them
and found them worthy.

Like gold in the furnace
God tried them, and,
like a sacrificial burnt offering,
accepted them.

In the time of their visitation
they will shine forth
and will run like sparks through the stubble.

They will govern nations
and rule over peoples
and God will reign over them for ever.

Give praise to the Father . . .

The Scripture Reading is read. See Lectionary tables (pages 4–18).

The Responsory (from Revelation 7:14)

V.   They have washed their robes in the blood of the Lamb.
R.   **They have washed their robes in the blood of the Lamb.**
V.   They have passed through great tribulation
R.   **in the blood of the Lamb.**
V.   Glory to the Father, the Son, the Holy Spirit.
R.   **They have washed their robes in the blood of the Lamb.**

Daily Prayer continues with the Canticle of the Season on page 102.

PASTORS (P)

The psalm(s) are said. See Lectionary tables (pages 4–18).

Canticle of the Day:
A Song of Faith and Hope (Romans 5:1, 3, 5, 8; 8:38, 39)

> Now that we have been justified through faith
> we are at peace with God
> through Jesus Christ our Lord.
>
> And so we exult
> in our hope of the splendour of God,
> and we even exult
> in the sufferings we endure.
>
> For our hope is not in vain
> because God's love has flooded our inmost hearts
> through the Holy Spirit which has been given to us.
>
> When we were still powerless,
> Christ died for the ungodly;
> he died for us while we were still sinners,
> and so God's love for us is revealed.
>
> We are more than conquerors
> through Christ who loved us,
> for nothing can separate us from the love of God
> which is ours, through Jesus Christ.
>
> Give praise to the Father . . .

The Scripture Reading is read. See Lectionary tables (pages 4–18).

The Responsory (from Psalm 37:31)

> V. The law of God was their guide, their minds were fixed on God.
> R. **The law of God was their guide, their minds were fixed on God.**
> V. Their steps did not falter,
> R. **their minds were fixed on God.**
> V. Glory to the Father, the Son, the Holy Spirit.
> R. **The law of God was their guide, their minds were fixed on God.**

Daily Prayer continues with the Canticle of the Season on page 102.

OTHERS (O)

The psalm(s) are said. See Lectionary tables (pages 4–18).

Canticle of the Day: A Song of the Redeemed (Revelation 7:9–10, 14b–17)

Behold, a great multitude
which no one could number,
from every nation,
from all tribes and peoples and tongues,
standing before the throne and the Lamb.

They were clothed in white robes
and had palms in their hands,
and they cried with a loud voice, saying,

'Salvation belongs to our God
who sits on the throne, and to the Lamb.'

These are they who have come out of the great tribulation,
they have washed their robes
and made them white in the blood of the Lamb.

Therefore they stand before the throne of God
whom they serve day and night within the temple;
and the One who sits upon the throne
will shelter them with his presence.

They shall never again feel hunger or thirst,
the sun shall not strike them, nor any scorching heat.

For the Lamb at the heart of the throne
will be their Shepherd;
he will guide them to springs of living water
and God will wipe away every tear from their eyes.

To the One who sits on the throne, and to the Lamb,
be blessing and honour and glory and might,
for ever and ever. Amen.

The Scripture Reading is read. See Lectionary tables (pages 4–18).

The Responsory (from Psalm 32:10)
V.   Rejoice in the Lord, let the just shout for joy.
R.   **Rejoice in the Lord, let the just shout for joy.**
V.   Let the upright sing praise,
R.   **let the just shout for joy.**
V.   Glory to the Father, the Son, the Holy Spirit.
R.   **Rejoice in the Lord, let the just shout for joy.**

Daily Prayer continues with the Canticle of the Season on page 102.

EVERY DAY

CANTICLE OF THE SEASON

A Song of the Church (Te Deum)

We praise you, O God,
we acclaim you as Lord;
all creation worships you,
the Father everlasting.

To you all angels, all the powers of heaven,
the cherubim and seraphim, sing in endless praise:

Holy, holy, holy Lord,
God of power and might,
heaven and earth are full of your glory.

The glorious company of apostles praise you.
The noble fellowship of prophets praise you.

The white-robed army of martyrs praise you.
Throughout the world the holy Church acclaims you:

Father, of majesty unbounded,
your true and only Son, worthy of all praise,
the Holy Spirit, advocate and guide.

You, Christ, are the king of glory,
the eternal Son of the Father.

When you took our flesh to set us free
you humbly chose the Virgin's womb.
You overcame the sting of death
and opened the kingdom of heaven to all believers.

You are seated at God's right hand in glory.
We believe that you will come to be our judge.

Come then, Lord, and help your people,
bought with the price of your own blood,
and bring us with your saints to glory everlasting.

PRAYER AND THANKSGIVING

The Lord's Prayer is said. It may be introduced by

Enlightened by the glory of God, we pray:
Our Father…

Specific intercessions and thanksgivings should be offered here.
These may begin with:

Today	its encounters, opportunities and demands.
Currently	concerns and achievements in our churches and society: locally, nationally and around the world.

A personal Prayer Diary or some other Cycle of Intercession may guide further prayer.

Prayer may also be offered using one or more of the following categories:

Local	Community life, work, leisure, education.
	The sick, the bereaved, the lonely.
	The witness and fellowship of God's people.
National	Government, commerce and industry, institutions.
	The unemployed, victims of crime, or marginalised.
	The Church: its leaders and its prophetic role.
Global	Nations and their leaders; justice, peace and development.
	Refugees and victims of war.
	The dispossessed, the hungry, the persecuted.
	The Church: its partnership in world mission.

The period of prayer is concluded with the following responses:

V.   In your glory, Lord, protect us by the power of your name:
R.   **that we may be one as you are one.**

V.   We are in the world but not of it:
R.   **protect us from the evil one.**

V.   Give us your word and the full measure of your joy:
R.   **sanctify us by your truth.**

V.   May your Spirit unite us in the love and glory of Father and Son:
R.   **may we be one that the world may believe.**

V.   As you sent your Son into the world:
R.   **so send us, to make your glory known.**

The collect of the festival should be said if available.

One or more of these Concluding Prayers is said, or another of your choice.

God of love and justice,
you make known your ways in the lives of your saints.
    Receive all we offer you this day,
    and help us to know your holy will and do it;
    through Jesus Christ our Lord. **Amen.**

Lord, make us instruments of your peace.
    Where there is hatred, let us sow love;
    where there is injury, let there be pardon;
    where there is discord, union;
    where there is doubt, faith;
    where there is despair, hope;
    where there is darkness, light;
    where there is sadness, joy;
for your mercy and for your truth's sake. **Amen.**

Grant us your light, O Lord.
Let it shine in the darkness of our hearts
    that at the last we may be brought
    to the true light which is Christ our Lord. **Amen.**

Lord Christ,
dwell in our hearts;
    that,
rooted and grounded in you
we may comprehend with all the saints
    what is the breadth and length
    and height and depth of your love,
    and be filled with all the fullness of God. **Amen.**

CONCLUSION

May the God of all grace who called us to his eternal glory in Christ Jesus, establish, strengthen and settle us in the faith. Amen.

Vigil of
the Resurrection

It is an ancient Jewish tradition that the Sabbath begins on the previous evening with a short act of (usually family) worship. This tradition was adopted by the early Christians who began their celebration of Sunday on Saturday evening. This brief act of worship is provided for those who wish to observe this tradition. It should be used in the late afternoon or early evening, before the evening meal. A lighted candle may be used to help focus on the risen Christ, the light of the world.

The basic structure of the *Vigil of the Resurrection* is the same as that of *Daily Prayer*, though some parts of the Order are omitted.

The hymn that is printed is particularly associated with this Vigil, though there are a number of alternative translations of it available in hymn books. A seasonal hymn may be used if preferred.

Four psalms are printed and these can be used according to the tables on the following pages or at the user's choice.

The Scripture reading is a Gospel of the Resurrection except during *The Season of Penitence*. This can be read according to the tables, and may be added to, or replaced by, the Gospel of the Sunday.

Four canticles are provided. The tables provide a scheme for using these that is appropriate to the season of the year while avoiding repetition of those set in *Daily Prayer*, but these also may be used at choice.

These tables provide a distribution of the psalms and Gospels of the Resurrection, with alternative Gospels given in Lent. It also avoids repetition of Canticles used in Daily Prayer in the various seasons. Your selection may be made according to this table, or as preferred. The Gospel of the Sunday may always be used in addition to or in place of the one given. The Sunday names are as used in the Church of England's calendar, 'The Christian Year', given within the seasons used in Daily Prayer.

Sunday	Psalm	Scripture	Canticle
THE SEASON OF JOYFUL HOPE			
4th Sunday before Advent	122	Mark 16:9–20	A
3rd Sunday before Advent	114	Luke 24:1–12	A
2nd Sunday before Advent	113	Luke 24:13–35	A
Christ the King – Year A	117	Matt. 28:16–20	A or B
Christ the King – Year B	117	Mark 16:15–20	A or B
Christ the King – Year C	117	Luke 24:44–53	A or B
1st Sunday of Advent	122	John 20:1–10	A
2nd Sunday of Advent	114	John 20:11–18	A
3rd Sunday of Advent	117	John 20:19–31	A
THE SEASON OF THE WORD MADE FLESH			
4th Sunday of Advent	113	John 21:1–14	A
1st Sunday of Christmas	113	Matt. 28:1–10, 16–20	D
2nd Sunday of Christmas	122	Mark 16:1–7	D
The Baptism of Christ	114	Mark 16:9–20	D
2nd Sunday of Epiphany	117	Luke 24:1–12	A or D
3rd Sunday of Epiphany	114	Luke 24:13–35	A or D
4th Sunday of Epiphany	113	Luke 24:35–53	A or D
THROUGH THE YEAR			
5th Sunday before Lent	122	John 20:1–10	A or D
4th Sunday before Lent	117	John 20:11–18	A or D
3rd Sunday before Lent	113	John 20:19–31	A or D
2nd Sunday before Lent	114	John 21:1–14	A or D
Sunday before Lent	117	John 21:15–25	A or D

PSALMS, LECTIONARY, and CANTICLES — VIGIL OF THE RESURRECTION

Sunday	Psalm	Scripture	Canticle
THE SEASON OF PENITENCE			
1st Sunday of Lent	122	Luke 18:9–14	C
2nd Sunday of Lent	117	Matt. 16:21–28	C
3rd Sunday of Lent	114	Mark 9:30–37	C
4th Sunday of Lent	117	Mark 10:32–45	C
5th Sunday of Lent	114	Mark 12:1–12	C
THE SEASON OF PASSION AND RESURRECTION			
Palm Sunday	122	John 2:13–22	C
Easter Day	*this is replaced by the Easter Vigil*		
2nd Sunday of Easter	113	Mark 16:1–7	B
THE SEASON OF NEW LIFE			
3rd Sunday of Easter	114	Mark 16:9–20	B
4th Sunday of Easter	122	Luke 24:1–12	B
5th Sunday of Easter	113	Luke 24:13–35	B
6th Sunday of Easter	114	Luke 24:35–48	B
Ascension Day	117	Matt. 28:16–20	B
7th Sunday of Easter	117	John 20:19–31	B
Day of Pentecost	122	Matt. 28:16–20	B
THROUGH THE YEAR			
Trinity Sunday	113	John 21:1–14	A
1st, 11th Sundays after Trinity	114	Matt. 28:1–10,16–20	A or D
2nd, 12th Sundays after Trinity	117	Mark 16:1–7	A or D
3rd, 13th Sundays after Trinity	122	Mark 16:9–20	A or D
4th, 14th Sundays after Trinity	113	Luke 24:1–12	A or D
5th, 15th Sundays after Trinity	114	Luke 24:13–35	A or D
6th, 16th Sundays after Trinity	117	Luke 24:35–53	A or D
7th, 17th Sundays after Trinity	122	John 20:1–10	A or D
8th, 18th Sundays after Trinity	113	John 20:11–18	A or D
9th, 19th Sundays after Trinity	114	John 20:19–31	A or D
10th, 20th Sundays after Trinity	117	John 21:1–14	A or D
21st Sunday after Trinity	122	Mark 16:1–7	A or D
Last Sunday after Trinity	113	Matt. 28:1–10,16–20	A or D

OPENING

All seasons, except Resurrection and New Life

    V.   This is the day the Lord made.
    R.   **Let us rejoice and be glad.**

**Give praise to the Father almighty,
to his Son, Jesus Christ, the Lord,
to the Spirit who dwells in our hearts,
both now and for ever. Amen.**

Alleluia! *(omitted in Lent)*

During the Seasons of Resurrection and New Life

    V.   We are an Easter people:
    R.   **Alleluia is our song!**

**Give praise to the Father almighty,
to his Son, Jesus Christ, the Lord,
to the Spirit who dwells in our hearts,
both now and for ever. Amen.**

Alleluia!

Hail, gladdening light,
of his pure glory poured
from the immortal Father,
heavenly, blest,
holiest of holies,
Jesus Christ our Lord.

Now we are come
to the sun's hour of rest,
the lights of evening
round us shine,
we hymn the Father,
Son and Holy Spirit divine.

Worthiest art thou at all time
to be sung with undefiled tongue,
Son of our God,
giver of life, alone:
therefore in all the world thy glories,
Lord, they own.

Opening Prayer

Blessed are you, God our Father,
you have enlightened us with the glory of everlasting life
and revealed the light that never fades.

A few words of extempore prayer may be added here

The darkness of death has been destroyed
and radiant life is now restored.
What you promised, you have fulfilled,
by raising Jesus from the dead and giving him glory.

Blessed be God for ever!

The psalm is said from those on the following pages.
See Lectionary table (pages 106–107).

Psalm 113 ('Alleluia!' is omitted in Lent)

Alleluia!

Praise, O servants of the Lord,
praise the name of the Lord!
May the name of the Lord be blessed
both now and for evermore!
From the rising of the sun to its setting
praised be the name of the Lord!

High above all nations is the Lord,
above the heavens God's glory.
Who is like the Lord, our God,
the one enthroned on high,
who stoops from the heights to look down,
to look down upon heaven and earth?

From the dust God lifts up the lowly,
from the dungheap God raises the poor
to set them in the company of rulers,
yes, with the rulers of the people.
To the childless wife God gives a home
and gladdens her heart with children.

Psalm 114 ('Alleluia!' is omitted in Lent)

Alleluia!

When Israel came forth from Egypt,
Jacob's family from an alien people,
Judah became the Lord's temple,
Israel became God's kingdom.

The sea fled at the sight,
the Jordan turned back on its course,
the mountains leapt like rams
and the hills like yearling sheep.

Why was it, sea, that you fled,
that you turned back, Jordan, on your course?
Mountains, that you leapt like rams;
hills, like yearling sheep?

Tremble, O earth, before the Lord,
in the presence of the God of Jacob,
who turns the rock into a pool
and flint into a spring of water.

Psalm 117 *('Alleluia!' is omitted in Lent)*

Alleluia!

O praise the Lord, all you nations,
acclaim God all you peoples!

Strong is God's love for us;
the Lord is faithful for ever.

Psalm 122

I rejoiced when I heard them say:
'Let us go to God's house.'
And now our feet are standing
within your gates, O Jerusalem.

Jerusalem is built as a city
strongly compact.
It is there that the tribes go up,
the tribes of the Lord.

For Israel's law it is,
there to praise the Lord's name.
There were set the thrones of judgement
of the house of David.

For the peace of Jerusalem pray:
'Peace be to your homes!
May peace reign in your walls,
in your palaces, peace!'

For the love of my family and friends
I say: 'Peace upon you.'
For love of the house of the Lord
I will ask for your good.

The Scripture Reading

The Gospel of the Resurrection may be read. See Lectionary table (pages 106–107).
Alternatively, or additionally, the Gospel of the Sunday may be read.

Responsory *(from 1 Peter 1:21)*

V.   God raised up Jesus; he gave him glory.
R.   **God raised up Jesus; he gave him glory.**
V.   That our faith and hope might be in God,
R.   **he gave him glory.**
V.   Glory to the Father, the Son, the Holy Spirit.
R.   **God raised up Jesus; he gave him glory.**

CANTICLE

One or more of the following canticles may be used. See Lectionary table (pages 106–107).

Then turn to page 114 for Prayer and Thanksgiving.

Canticle A: The Easter Anthems
(1 Corinthians 5:7–8; Romans 6:9–11; 1 Corinthians 15:20–22)

Christ our passover has been sacrificed for us
so let us celebrate the feast:
not with the old leaven of corruption and wickedness,
but with the unleavened bread of sincerity and truth.

Christ once raised from the dead dies no more,
death has no more dominion over him.
In dying he died to sin once for all,
in living he lives to God.

See yourselves therefore as dead to sin,
and alive to God in Jesus Christ our Lord.

Christ has been raised from the dead,
the first fruits of those who sleep.

For since by one man came death
by another has come also the resurrection of the dead;
for as in Adam all die,
even so in Christ shall all be made alive.

Canticle B: The Easter Song of Praise (Exsultet)

Rejoice, heavenly powers! Sing, choirs of angels!
Exult, all creation around God's throne!
Jesus Christ, our King, is risen!
Sound the trumpet of salvation!

Rejoice, O earth, in shining splendour,
radiant in the brightness of your King!
Christ has conquered! Glory fills you!
Darkness vanishes for ever!

Rejoice, O Mother Church! Exult in glory!
The risen Saviour shines upon you!
Let this place resound with joy,
echoing the mighty song of all God's people!

Canticle C: Slavonic Hymn of the Resurrection

Having beheld the resurrection of Christ,
let us adore the holy Lord Jesus, the only sinless one.

We venerate your cross, O Christ,
your holy resurrection we laud and glorify.

For you are our God and we know no other beside you;
we call upon your name.

Come all you faithful, let us magnify Christ's holy resurrection;
for behold, through the cross joy has come into all the world.

Ever blessing the Lord, let us sing his resurrection,
for us he endured the shame of the cross, conquering death by his death.

Canticle D: A Song of the Church (Te Deum)

We praise you, O God,
we acclaim you as Lord;
all creation worships you,
the Father everlasting.

To you all angels, all the powers of heaven,
the cherubim and seraphim, sing in endless praise:

> Holy, holy, holy Lord,
> God of power and might,
> heaven and earth are full of your glory.

The glorious company of apostles praise you.
The noble fellowship of prophets praise you.

The white-robed army of martyrs praise you.
Throughout the world the holy Church acclaims you:

> Father, of majesty unbounded,
> your true and only Son, worthy of all praise,
> the Holy Spirit, advocate and guide.

You, Christ, are the king of glory,
the eternal Son of the Father.

When you took our flesh to set us free
you humbly chose the Virgin's womb.
You overcame the sting of death
and opened the kingdom of heaven to all believers.

You are seated at God's right hand in glory.
We believe that you will come to be our judge.

Come then, Lord, and help your people,
bought with the price of your own blood,
and bring us with your saints to glory everlasting.

PRAYER AND THANKSGIVING

The Lord's Prayer is said. It may be introduced by

> Delivered and made new in Christ, we pray:
> Our Father . . .

The collect of the Sunday should be said if available,
then one of these Concluding Prayers.

> Light and life of the world, Lord Jesus Christ,
> > keep the joy of Easter alive in us always.
> Let your light shine forth from us
> > that we may be witnesses to your resurrection
> > and heirs to eternal life in your kingdom,
> where you are alive and reign for ever and ever. **Amen**.

> Kindle in our hearts, O God, *(especially in Lent)*
> > the flame of that love which never ceases,
> > that it may burn in us, giving light to others.
> May we shine for ever in your temple,
> > set on fire with your eternal light,
> Jesus Christ, our Saviour and Redeemer. **Amen**.

> You are risen — Let trumpets proclaim.
> You are risen — Let sun brightly flame.
> You are risen — Dark night is past.
> You are risen — Hope will now last.
> You are risen — Let us not dread.
> You are risen — Back from the dead.
> You are risen — Lord of the skies.
> You are risen — Help us to rise.

> Risen Lord, *(not in Lent)*
> > give us a heart for simple things;
> > > love, laughter, bread, wine and dreams.
> Fill us with green, growing hope
> > and make us a people
> > > whose song is Hallelujah;
> > > whose sign is Peace
> > > and whose name is Love. **Amen**.

CONCLUSION

Christ is risen indeed from the dead. Glory and power are his for ever and ever. Amen.

Prayer
Through the Day

Prayer in the Morning and *Prayer in the Evening* are intended to supplement *Daily Prayer* for those who wish to add brief times of prayer at the start and end of the day, while setting aside time elsewhere in the day for their main prayer and worship. The psalms used also occur in the cycle of psalmody in *Daily Prayer* so that anyone using only Daily Prayer without the supplements will not be omitting any essential material.

Those newly introduced to regular daily prayer may initially wish to use these supplements on their own without *Daily Prayer*. Though such use will sanctify the day with prayer, the user will get a very restricted diet of psalmody and Scripture and we would hope that before long they might be encouraged to begin using *Daily Prayer* as well or instead.

Christian groups may also find these short acts of worship useful where there is a desire to do more than say a simple prayer at the beginning or end of a meeting.

This section contains the minimum material for this form of prayer. It can be supplemented by the addition of other material such as a hymn, or a longer Scripture reading.

The basic structure of *Prayer in the Morning* and *Prayer in the Evening* is the same as that of *Daily Prayer*, though some parts of the Order are omitted. In addition to provision for each day of the week, extra provision is made for Saints' and Holy Days on pages 160f. Fuller notes are given in the Commentary.

Sunday's order can be used on any day and may be committed to memory for those times when no material is available.

The daily pages headed *During the Day* are intended to be used within the context of *Daily Prayer* in place of the psalms and readings set in the Lectionary tables. This may be particularly useful when travelling, or on any other occasion where a Bible and Psalter are not available. They may also be used as an alternative to those given for *Prayer in the Morning* to provide greater variety by using them as a fortnightly cycle.

OPENING – MORNING

V.   Bless God's name for ever!
R.   **Let God's glory fill the world!**

**Give praise to the Father almighty,
to his Son, Jesus Christ, the Lord,
to the Spirit who dwells in our hearts,
both now and for ever. Amen.**

Alleluia! *(omitted in Lent)*

A hymn, or one of these, or another acclamation may be sung

Come into his presence, singing,
'Alleluia. Alleluia. Alleluia.'   *(not this verse in Lent)*

Come into his presence, singing,
'Jesus is Lord. Jesus is Lord. Jesus is Lord.'

Come into his presence, singing,
'Glory to God. Glory to God. Glory to God.'

Gloria, gloria in excelsis Deo!
Gloria, gloria, alleluia, alleluia!   *(not in Lent)*

In the Lord I'll be ever thankful,
in the Lord, I will rejoice!
Look to God, do not be afraid;
lift up your voices: the Lord is near,
lift up your voices, the Lord is near.

Prayer in the Morning continues on the following pages according to the day of the week.

OPENING – EVENING

V.   We sing God's love all our days,
R.   **God's faithfulness, from age to age.**

**Give praise to the Father almighty,
to his Son, Jesus Christ, the Lord,
to the Spirit who dwells in our hearts,
both now and for ever. Amen.**

Alleluia! *(omitted in Lent)*

A hymn, or one of these, or another acclamation may be sung

> Calm me, Lord, as you calmed the storm;
> still me, Lord, keep me from harm.
> Let all the tumult within me cease;
> enfold me, Lord, in your peace.

> *'Nada te turbe'*
> Nothing can trouble,
> nothing can frighten.
> Those who seek God shall never go wanting.
> Nothing can trouble,
> nothing can frighten.
> God alone fills us.

> The Lord is my song, the Lord is my praise:
> all my hope comes from God.
> The Lord is my song, the Lord is my praise:
> God the well-spring of life.

*Prayer in the Evening continues on the following pages according to the day
of the week.*

SUNDAY MORNING

Psalm 150 ('Alleluia!' is omitted in Lent)
>Alleluia!

Praise God in his holy place,
sing praise in the mighty heavens.
Sing praise for God's powerful deeds,
praise God's surpassing greatness.

Sing praise with sound of trumpet,
sing praise with lute and harp.
Sing praise with timbrel and dance,
sing praise with strings and pipes.

Sing praise with resounding cymbals,
sing praise with clashing of cymbals.
Let everything that lives and that breathes
give praise to the Lord. Alleluia!

The Scripture Reading from the selection on the facing page.

Responsory (from Psalm 71:23, 24)

V. I will sing out with joy, I will sing of how you saved me.
R. **I will sing out with joy, I will sing of how you saved me.**
V. From morning till night
R. **I will sing of how you saved me.**
V. Glory to the Father, the Son, the Holy Spirit.
R. **I will sing out with joy, I will sing of how you saved me.**

Prayer in the Morning concludes on page 166.

Through the Year: Revelation 7:10–11

The multitude cried out in a loud voice, saying, 'Salvation belongs to our God who is seated on the throne, and to the Lamb!' And all the angels stood around the throne and around the elders and the four living creatures, and they fell on their faces before the throne and worshipped God.

Joyful Hope: Philippians 4:4–5

Rejoice in the Lord always; again I will say, Rejoice. Let your gentleness be known to everyone. The Lord is near.

Word Made Flesh: 1 John 1:1–3

We declare to you what was from the beginning, what we have heard, what we have seen with our eyes, what we have looked at and touched with our hands, concerning the word of life – this life was revealed, and we have seen it and testify to it, and declare to you the eternal life that was with the Father and was revealed to us – we declare to you what we have seen and heard so that you also may have fellowship with us; and truly our fellowship is with the Father and with his Son Jesus Christ.

Penitence: Isaiah 1:16–18

Wash yourselves; make yourselves clean; remove the evil of your doings from before my eyes; cease to do evil, learn to do good; seek justice, rescue the oppressed, defend the orphan, plead for the widow. Come now, let us argue it out, says the Lord: though your sins are like scarlet, they shall be like snow; though they are red like crimson, they shall become like wool.

Palm Sunday: Zechariah 9:9

Rejoice greatly, O daughter Zion! Shout aloud, O daughter Jerusalem! Lo, your king comes to you; triumphant and victorious is he, humble and riding on a donkey, on a colt, the foal of a donkey.

Resurrection and New Life : John 6:51a, 54–57

Jesus said, 'I am the living bread that came down from heaven. Those who eat my flesh and drink my blood have eternal life, and I will raise them up on the last day; for my flesh is true food and my blood is true drink. Those who eat my flesh and drink my blood abide in me, and I in them. Just as the living Father sent me, and I live because of the Father, so whoever eats me will live because of me.'

Pentecost: 1 Corinthians 2:9–10

What no eye has seen, nor ear heard, nor the human heart conceived, what God has prepared for those who love him – these things God has revealed to us through the Spirit; for the Spirit searches everything, even the depths of God.

SUNDAY DURING THE DAY

Psalm 84

> How lovely is your dwelling place,
> Lord, God of hosts.
>
> My soul is longing and yearning,
> is yearning for the courts of the Lord.
> My heart and my soul ring out their joy
> to God, the living God.
>
> The sparrow herself finds a home
> and the swallow a nest for her brood;
> she lays her young by your altars,
> Lord of hosts, my king and my God.
>
> They are happy, who dwell in your house,
> for ever singing your praise.
> They are happy, whose strength is in you,
> in whose hearts are the roads to Zion.
>
> As they go through the Bitter Valley
> they make it a place of springs,
> the autumn rain covers it with blessings.
> They walk with ever growing strength,
> they will see the God of gods in Zion.
>
> O Lord God of hosts, hear my prayer,
> give ear, O God of Jacob.
> Turn your eyes, O God, our shield,
> look on the face of your anointed.
>
> One day within your courts
> is better than a thousand elsewhere.
> The threshold of the house of God
> I prefer to the dwellings of the wicked.
>
> For the Lord God is a rampart, a shield.
> The Lord will give us favour and glory.
> The Lord will not refuse any good
> to those who walk without blame.
>
> Lord, God of hosts,
> happy are those who trust in you!

Through the Year: Ezekiel 36:25–27

I will sprinkle clean water upon you, and you shall be clean from all your unclean-nesses, and from all your idols I will cleanse you. A new heart I will give you, and a new spirit I will put within you; and I will remove from your body the heart of stone and give you a heart of flesh. I will put my spirit within you, and make you follow my statutes and be careful to observe my ordinances.

Joyful Hope: Mark 1:14b–15

Jesus came to Galilee, proclaiming the good news of God, and saying, 'The time is fulfilled, and the kingdom of God has come near; repent, and believe in the good news.'

Word Made Flesh: John 1:9–13

The true light, which enlightens everyone, was coming into the world. He was in the world, and the world came into being through him; yet the world did not know him. He came to what was his own, and his own people did not accept him. But to all who received him, who believed in his name, he gave power to become children of God, who were born, not of blood or of the will of the flesh or of the will of man, but of God.

Penitence: 2 Corinthians 6:1–4a

As we work together with Christ, we urge you also not to accept the grace of God in vain. For he says, 'At an acceptable time I have listened to you, and on a day of sal-vation I have helped you.' See, now is the acceptable time; see, now is the day of sal-vation! We are putting no obstacle in anyone's way, so that no fault may be found with our ministry, but as servants of God we have commended ourselves in every way.

Resurrection and New Life: Luke 24:5b–7

Why do you look for the living among the dead? He is not here, but has risen. Remember how he told you, while he was still in Galilee, that the Son of Man must be handed over to sinners, and be crucified, and on the third day rise again.

Pentecost: Romans 8:26–27

The Spirit helps us in our weakness; for we do not know how to pray as we ought, but that very Spirit intercedes with sighs too deep for words. And God, who searches the heart, knows what is the mind of the Spirit, because the Spirit intercedes for the saints according to the will of God.

SUNDAY EVENING

Psalm 91:1–7, 10–11, 14–16

Those who dwell in the shelter of the Most High
and abide in the shade of the Almighty
say to the Lord: 'My refuge,
my stronghold, my God in whom I trust!'

It is God who will free you from the snare
of the fowler who seeks to destroy you;
God will conceal you with his pinions,
and under his wings you will find refuge.

You will not fear the terror of the night
nor the arrow that flies by day,
nor the plague that prowls in the darkness
nor the scourge that lays waste at noon.

A thousand may fall at your side,
ten thousand fall at your right,
you, it will never approach;
God's faithfulness is buckler and shield.

Upon you no evil shall fall,
no plague approach where you dwell.
For you God has commanded the angels,
to keep you in all your ways.

You set your love on me so I will save you,
protect you for you know my name.
When you call I shall answer: 'I am with you,'
I will save you in distress and give you glory.

With length of days I will content you;
I shall let you see my saving power.

The Scripture Reading from the selection on the facing page.

Responsory (from Psalm 77:12, 13)

 V. I recall your awesome deeds, your wonders of old.
 R. **I recall your awesome deeds, your wonders of old.**
 V. I reflect on all your works,
 R. **your wonders of old.**
 V. Glory to the Father, the Son, the Holy Spirit.
 R. **I recall your awesome deeds, your wonders of old.**

Prayer in the Evening concludes on page 167.

Through the Year: Revelation 22:4–5

The servants of God will see his face, and his name will be on their foreheads. And there will be no more night; they need no light of lamp or sun, for the Lord God will be their light, and they will reign for ever and ever.

Joyful Hope: Romans 8:26–27

The Spirit helps us in our weakness; for we do not know how to pray as we ought, but that very Spirit intercedes with sighs too deep for words. And God, who searches the heart, knows what is the mind of the Spirit, because the Spirit intercedes for the saints according to the will of God.

Word Made Flesh: Isaiah 9:6

A child has been born for us, a son given to us; authority rests upon his shoulders; and he is named Wonderful Counsellor, Mighty God, Everlasting Father, Prince of Peace.

Penitence: Exodus 19:4–6a

You have seen what I did to the Egyptians, and how I bore you on eagles' wings and brought you to myself. Now therefore, if you obey my voice and keep my covenant, you shall be my treasured possession out of all the peoples. Indeed, the whole earth is mine, but you shall be for me a priestly kingdom and a holy nation.

Palm Sunday: Acts 13:26b–30

To us the message of this salvation has been sent. Because the residents of Jerusalem and their leaders did not recognize Jesus or understand the words of the prophets that are read every sabbath, they fulfilled those words by condemning him. Even though they found no cause for a sentence of death, they asked Pilate to have him killed. When they had carried out everything that was written about him, they took him down from the tree and laid him in a tomb. But God raised him from the dead.

Resurrection and New Life: Luke 24:29–31a

They urged him strongly, saying, 'Stay with us, because it is almost evening and the day is now nearly over.' So he went in to stay with them. When he was at the table with them, he took bread, blessed and broke it, and gave it to them. Then their eyes were opened, and they recognized him.

Pentecost: John 20:21–23

Jesus said to the disciples, 'Peace be with you. As the Father has sent me, so I send you.' When he had said this, he breathed on them and said to them, 'Receive the Holy Spirit. If you forgive the sins of any, they are forgiven them; if you retain the sins of any, they are retained.'

MONDAY MORNING

Psalm 19:1–5, 7–11, 15

> The heavens proclaim the glory of God,
> and the firmament shows forth the work of God's hands.
> Day unto day takes up the story
> and night unto night makes known the message.
>
> No speech, no word, no voice is heard
> yet their span extends through all the earth,
> their words to the utmost bounds of the world.
>
> At the end of the sky is the rising of the sun;
> to the furthest end of the sky is its course.
> There is nothing concealed from its burning heat.
>
> The law of the Lord is perfect,
> it revives the soul.
> The rule of the Lord is to be trusted,
> it gives wisdom to the simple.
>
> The precepts of the Lord are right,
> they gladden the heart.
> The command of the Lord is clear,
> it gives light to the eyes.
>
> The fear of the Lord is holy,
> abiding for ever.
> The decrees of the Lord are truth
> and all of them just.
>
> They are more to be desired than gold,
> than the purest of gold
> and sweeter are they than honey,
> than honey from the comb.
>
> May the spoken words of my mouth,
> the thoughts of my heart,
> win favour in your sight, O Lord,
> my rescuer, my rock!

The Scripture Reading from the selection on the facing page.

Responsory (from Psalm 9:2, 3)

> V. With a heart full of thanks I proclaim your wonders.
> R. **With a heart full of thanks I proclaim your wonders.**
> V. You are my joy and my delight,
> R. **I proclaim your wonders.**
> V. Glory to the Father, the Son, the Holy Spirit.
> R. **With a heart full of thanks I proclaim your wonders.**

Prayer in the Morning concludes on page 166.

Through the Year: Matthew 5:13–16

You are the salt of the earth; but if salt has lost its taste, how can its saltiness be restored? It is no longer good for anything, but is thrown out and trampled under foot. You are the light of the world. A city built on a hill cannot be hidden. No one after lighting a lamp puts it under the bushel basket, but on the lampstand, and it gives light to all in the house. In the same way, let your light shine before others, so that they may see your good works and give glory to your Father in heaven.

Joyful Hope: Isaiah 45:8

Shower, O heavens, from above, and let the skies rain down righteousness; let the earth open, that salvation may spring up, and let it cause righteousness to sprout up also; I the Lord have created it.

Word Made Flesh: Acts 10:37–38

The message spread throughout Judea, beginning in Galilee after the baptism that John announced: how God anointed Jesus of Nazareth with the Holy Spirit and with power; how he went about doing good and healing all who were oppressed by the devil, for God was with him.

Penitence: Matthew 6:19–21, 24

Do not store up for yourselves treasures on earth, where moth and rust consume and where thieves break in and steal; but store up for yourselves treasures in heaven, where neither moth nor rust consumes and where thieves do not break in and steal. For where your treasure is, there your heart will be also. No one can serve two masters; for a slave will either hate the one and love the other, or be devoted to the one and despise the other. You cannot serve God and wealth.

Passion: Isaiah 50:6–7

I gave my back to those who struck me, and my cheeks to those who pulled out the beard; I did not hide my face from insult and spitting. The Lord God helps me; therefore I have not been disgraced; therefore I have set my face like flint, and I know that I shall not be put to shame.

Resurrection and New Life: Romans 10:8–10

The word is near you, on your lips and in your heart (that is, the word of faith that we proclaim); because if you confess with your lips that Jesus is Lord and believe in your heart that God raised him from the dead, you will be saved. For one believes with the heart and so is justified, and one confesses with the mouth and so is saved.

MONDAY DURING THE DAY

Psalm 119:1–8, 169–176

They are happy whose life is blameless,
who follow God's law!
They are happy who do God's will,
seeking God with all their hearts,
who never do anything evil
but walk in God's ways.

You have laid down your precepts
to be obeyed with care.
May my footsteps be firm
to obey your statutes.
Then I shall not be put to shame
as I heed your commands.

I will thank you with an upright heart
as I learn your decrees.
I will obey your statutes;
do not forsake me.

Lord, let my cry come before you:
teach me by your word.
Let my pleading come before you:
save me by your promise.

Let my lips proclaim your praise
because you teach me your statutes.
Let my tongue sing your promise
for your commands are just.

Let your hand be ready to help me,
since I have chosen your precepts.
Lord, I long for your saving help
and your law is my delight.

Give life to my soul that I may praise you.
Let your decrees give me help.
I am lost like a sheep; seek your servant
for I remember your commands.

Through the Year: John 8:12

Jesus spoke to them, saying, 'I am the light of the world. Whoever follows me will never walk in darkness but will have the light of life.'

Joyful Hope: Isaiah 62:11–12

The Lord has proclaimed to the end of the earth: Say to daughter Zion, 'See, your salvation comes; his reward is with him, and his recompense before him.' They shall be called, 'The Holy People, The Redeemed of the Lord'; and you shall be called, 'Sought Out, A City Not Forsaken.'

Word Made Flesh: 1 John 1:5b–7

God is light and in him there is no darkness at all. If we say that we have fellowship with him while we are walking in darkness, we lie and do not do what is true; but if we walk in the light as he himself is in the light, we have fellowship with one another, and the blood of Jesus his Son cleanses us from all sin.

Penitence: 1 Corinthians 1:27–30

God chose what is foolish in the world to shame the wise; God chose what is weak in the world to shame the strong; God chose what is low and despised in the world, things that are not, to reduce to nothing things that are, so that no one might boast in the presence of God. He is the source of your life in Christ Jesus, who became for us wisdom from God, and righteousness and sanctification and redemption.

Resurrection and New Life: Colossians 3:1

If you have been raised with Christ, seek the things that are above, where Christ is, seated at the right hand of God.

MONDAY EVENING

Psalm 4

When I call, answer me, O God of justice;
from anguish you released me, have mercy and hear me!

You rebels, how long will your hearts be closed,
will you love what is futile and seek what is false?

It is the Lord who grants favours to those who are merciful;
the Lord who hears me whenever I call.

Tremble; do not sin: ponder on your bed and be still.
Make justice your sacrifice and trust in the Lord.

'What can bring us happiness?' many say.
Lift up the light of your face on us, O Lord.

You have put into my heart a greater joy
than they have from abundance of corn and new wine.

I will lie down in peace and sleep comes at once
for you alone, Lord, make me dwell in safety.

The Scripture Reading from the selection on the facing page.

Responsory (from Psalm 17:8, 9)

V. Keep a loving eye on me, guard me under your wings.
R. **Keep a loving eye on me, guard me under your wings.**
V. Hide me from those who attack,
R. **guard me under your wings.**
V. Glory to the Father, the Son, the Holy Spirit.
R. **Keep a loving eye on me, guard me under your wings.**

Prayer in the Evening concludes on page 167.

Through the Year: Jeremiah 14:9

Why should you be like someone confused, like a mighty warrior who cannot give help? Yet you, O Lord, are in the midst of us, and we are called by your name; do not forsake us!

Joyful Hope: Isaiah 49:8–9

Thus says the Lord: In a time of favour I have answered you, on a day of salvation I have helped you; I have kept you and given you as a covenant to the people, to establish the land, to apportion the desolate heritages; saying to the prisoners, 'Come out', to those who are in darkness, 'Show yourselves.' They shall feed along the ways, on all the bare heights shall be their pasture.

Word Made Flesh: Matthew 1:20b–21

An angel of the Lord appeared to Joseph in a dream and said, 'Joseph, son of David, do not be afraid to take Mary as your wife, for the child conceived in her is from the Holy Spirit. She will bear a son, and you are to name him Jesus, for he will save his people from their sins.'

Penitence: 2 Corinthians 12:9–10

The Lord said to me, 'My grace is sufficient for you, for power is made perfect in weakness.' So, I will boast all the more gladly of my weaknesses, so that the power of Christ may dwell in me. Therefore I am content with weaknesses, insults, hardships, persecutions, and calamities for the sake of Christ; for whenever I am weak, then I am strong.

Passion: Jeremiah 11:19–20

I was like a gentle lamb led to the slaughter. And I did not know it was against me that they devised schemes, saying, 'Let us destroy the tree with its fruit, let us cut him off from the land of the living, so that his name will no longer be remembered!' But you, O Lord of hosts, who judge righteously, who try the heart and the mind, let me see your retribution upon them, for to you I have committed my cause.

Resurrection and New Life: 1 Peter 1:18–21

You know that you were ransomed from the futile ways inherited from your ancestors, not with perishable things like silver or gold, but with the precious blood of Christ, like that of a lamb without defect or blemish. He was destined before the foundation of the world, but was revealed at the end of the ages for your sake. Through him you have come to trust in God, who raised him from the dead and gave him glory, so that your faith and hope are set on God.

TUESDAY MORNING

Psalm 93

> The Lord is king, with majesty enrobed;
> the Lord is robed with might,
> and girded round with power.
>
> The world you made firm, not to be moved;
> your throne has stood firm from of old.
> From all eternity, O Lord, you are.
>
> The waters have lifted up, O Lord,
> the waters have lifted up their voice,
> the waters have lifted up their thunder.
>
> Greater than the roar of mighty waters,
> more glorious than the surgings of the sea,
> the Lord is glorious on high.
>
> Truly your decrees are to be trusted.
> Holiness is fitting to your house,
> O Lord, until the end of time.

The Scripture Reading from the selection on the facing page.

Responsory (from Psalm 75:2)

    V.   We praise you, God, we give you thanks.
    R.   **We praise you, God, we give you thanks.**
    V.   We tell your wonders,
    R.   **we give you thanks.**
    V.   Glory to the Father, the Son, the Holy Spirit.
    R.   **We praise you, God, we give you thanks.**

Prayer in the Morning concludes on page 166.

Through the Year: Micah 6:6–7a, 8

With what shall I come before the Lord, and bow myself before God on high? Shall I come before him with burnt offerings, with calves a year old? Will the Lord be pleased with thousands of rams, with tens of thousands of rivers of oil? He has told you, O mortal, what is good; and what does the Lord require of you but to do justice, and to love kindness, and to walk humbly with your God?

Joyful Hope: James 5:7–9

Be patient, beloved, until the coming of the Lord. The farmer waits for the precious crop from the earth, being patient with it until it receives the early and the late rains. You also must be patient. Strengthen your hearts, for the coming of the Lord is near. Beloved, do not grumble against one another, so that you may not be judged. See, the Judge is standing at the doors!

Word Made Flesh: 2 Corinthians 8:9

You know the generous act of our Lord Jesus Christ, that though he was rich, yet for your sakes he became poor, so that by his poverty you might become rich.

Penitence: Galatians 2:19–20

Through the law I died to the law, so that I might live to God. I have been crucified with Christ; and it is no longer I who live, but it is Christ who lives in me. And the life I now live in the flesh I live by faith in the Son of God, who loved me and gave himself for me.

Passion: Hebrews 2:9–10

We see Jesus, who for a little while was made lower than the angels, now crowned with glory and honour because of the suffering of death, so that by the grace of God he might taste death for everyone. It was fitting that God, for whom and through whom all things exist, in bringing many children to glory, should make the pioneer of their salvation perfect through sufferings.

Resurrection and New Life: Acts 10:40–43

God raised Jesus on the third day and allowed him to appear, not to all the people but to us who were chosen by God as witnesses, and who ate and drank with him after he rose from the dead. He commanded us to preach to the people and to testify that he is the one ordained by God as judge of the living and the dead. All the prophets testify about him that everyone who believes in him receives forgiveness of sins through his name.

TUESDAY DURING THE DAY

Psalm 8

How great is your name, O Lord our God,
through all the earth!

Your majesty is praised above the heavens;
on the lips of children and of babes
you have found praise to foil your enemy,
to silence the foe and the rebel.

When I see the heavens, the work of your hands,
the moon and the stars which you arranged,
what are we that you should keep us in mind,
mere mortals that you care for us?

Yet you have made us little less than gods;
and crowned us with glory and honour,
you gave us power over the work of your hands,
put all things under our feet.

All of them, sheep and cattle,
yes, even the savage beasts,
birds of the air, and fish
that make their way through the waters.

How great is your name, O Lord our God,
through all the earth!

Through the Year: John 4:23–24

The hour is coming, and is now here, when the true worshippers will worship the Father in spirit and truth, for the Father seeks such as these to worship him. God is spirit, and those who worship him must worship in spirit and truth.

Joyful Hope: 1 Corinthians 1:8–9

God will strengthen you to the end, so that you may be blameless on the day of our Lord Jesus Christ. God is faithful; by him you were called into the fellowship of his Son, Jesus Christ our Lord.

Word Made Flesh: Luke 2:10–11

The angel said, 'Do not be afraid; for see – I am bringing you good news of great joy for all the people: to you is born this day in the city of David a Saviour, who is the Messiah, the Lord.'

Penitence: Isaiah 45:22–24

Turn to me and be saved, all the ends of the earth! For I am God, and there is no other. By myself I have sworn, from my mouth has gone forth in righteousness a word that shall not return: 'To me every knee shall bow, every tongue shall swear.' Only in the Lord, it shall be said of me, are righteousness and strength; all who were incensed against him shall come to him and be ashamed.

Resurrection and New Life: 1 Corinthians 15:3–4

I handed on to you as of first importance what I in turn had received: that Christ died for our sins in accordance with the scriptures, and that he was buried, and that he was raised on the third day in accordance with the scriptures.

TUESDAY EVENING

Psalm 16

Preserve me, God, I take refuge in you.
I say to you Lord: 'You are my God.
My happiness lies in you alone.'

You have put into my heart a marvellous love
for the faithful ones who dwell in your land.
Those who choose other gods increase their sorrows.
Never will I offer their offerings of blood.
Never will I take their name upon my lips.

O Lord, it is you who are my portion and cup,
it is you yourself who are my prize.
The lot marked out for me is my delight,
welcome indeed the heritage that falls to me!

I will bless you, Lord, you give me counsel,
and even at night direct my heart.
I keep you, Lord, ever in my sight;
since you are at my right hand, I shall stand firm.

And so my heart rejoices, my soul is glad;
even my body shall rest in safety.
For you will not leave my soul among the dead,
nor let your beloved know decay.

You will show me the path of life,
the fullness of joy in your presence,
at your right hand happiness for ever.

The Scripture Reading from the selection on the facing page.

Responsory (from Psalm 138:1, 2)

V.   I thank you with all I am, I join heaven's chorus.
R.   **I thank you with all I am, I join heaven's chorus.**
V.   I bow towards your holy temple to praise your name,
R.   **I join heaven's chorus.**
V.   Glory to the Father, the Son, the Holy Spirit.
R.   **I thank you with all I am, I join heaven's chorus.**

Prayer in the Evening concludes on page 167.

Through the Year: 1 Peter 5:8–9

Discipline yourselves; keep alert. Like a roaring lion your adversary the devil prowls around, looking for someone to devour. Resist him, steadfast in your faith, for you know that your brothers and sisters throughout the world are undergoing the same kinds of suffering.

Joyful Hope: Romans 12:14–16

Bless those who persecute you; bless and do not curse them. Rejoice with those who rejoice, weep with those who weep. Live in harmony with one another; do not be haughty, but associate with the lowly; do not claim to be wiser than you are.

Word Made Flesh: Hebrews 1:1–2

Long ago God spoke to our ancestors in many and various ways by the prophets, but in these last days he has spoken to us by a Son, whom he appointed heir of all things, through whom he also created the worlds.

Penitence: Matthew 7:21

Jesus said, 'Not everyone who says to me, "Lord, Lord", will enter the kingdom of heaven, but only one who does the will of my Father in heaven.'

Passion: Romans 5:8–9

God proves his love for us in that while we still were sinners Christ died for us. Much more surely then, now that we have been justified by his blood, will we be saved through him from the wrath of God.

Resurrection and New Life: John 4:14

Jesus said, 'Those who drink of the water that I will give them will never be thirsty. The water that I will give will become in them a spring of water gushing up to eternal life.'

WEDNESDAY MORNING

Psalm 126

> When the Lord delivered Zion from bondage,
> it seemed like a dream.
> Then was our mouth filled with laughter,
> on our lips there were songs.
>
> The heathens themselves said: 'What marvels
> the Lord worked for them!'
> What marvels the Lord worked for us!
> Indeed we were glad.
>
> Deliver us, O Lord, from our bondage
> as streams in dry land.
> Those who are sowing in tears
> will sing when they reap.
>
> They go out, they go out, full of tears,
> carrying seed for the sowing;
> they come back, they come back, full of song,
> carrying their sheaves.

The Scripture Reading from the selection on the facing page.

Responsory (from Psalm 92:2, 3)

> V.   How good to thank you, Lord, to praise your name, Most High.
> R.   **How good to thank you, Lord, to praise your name, Most High.**
> V.   To sing your love at dawn,
> R.   **to praise your name, Most High.**
> V.   Glory to the Father, the Son, the Holy Spirit.
> R.   **How good to thank you, Lord, to praise your name, Most High.**

Prayer in the Morning concludes on page 166.

Through the Year: 1 John 3:1–2
See what love the Father has given us, that we should be called children of God; and that is what we are. The reason the world does not know us is that it did not know him. Beloved, we are God's children now; what we will be has not yet been revealed. What we do know is this: when he is revealed, we will be like him, for we will see him as he is.

Joyful Hope: Isaiah 11:1–2
A shoot shall come out from the stock of Jesse, and a branch shall grow out of his roots. The spirit of the Lord shall rest on him, the spirit of wisdom and understanding, the spirit of counsel and might, the spirit of knowledge and the fear of the Lord.

Word Made Flesh: 1 John 5:20
We know that the Son of God has come and has given us understanding so that we may know him who is true; and we are in him who is true, in his Son Jesus Christ. He is the true God and eternal life.

Penitence: Joel 2:12–13
Even now, says the Lord, return to me with all your heart, with fasting, with weeping, and with mourning; rend your hearts and not your clothing. Return to the Lord, your God, for he is gracious and merciful, slow to anger, and abounding in steadfast love, and relents from punishing.

Passion: Isaiah 52:13–15
My servant shall prosper; he shall be exalted and lifted up, and shall be very high. Just as there were many who were astonished at him – so marred was his appearance, beyond human semblance, and his form beyond that of mortals – so he shall startle many nations; kings shall shut their mouths because of him; for that which had not been told them they shall see, and that which they had not heard they shall contemplate.

Resurrection and New Life: Romans 6:8–11
If we have died with Christ, we believe that we will also live with him. We know that Christ, being raised from the dead, will never die again; death no longer has dominion over him. The death he died, he died to sin, once for all; but the life he lives, he lives to God. So you also must consider yourselves dead to sin and alive to God in Christ Jesus.

WEDNESDAY DURING THE DAY

Psalm 146 ('Alleluia!' is omitted in Lent)

Alleluia!

My soul, give praise to the Lord;
I will praise the Lord all my days,
make music to my God while I live.

Put no trust in the powerful,
mere mortals in whom there is no help.
Take their breath, they return to clay
and their plans that day come to nothing.

They are happy who are helped by Jacob's God,
whose hope is in the Lord their God,
who alone made heaven and earth,
the seas and all they contain.

It is the Lord who keeps faith for ever,
who is just to those who are oppressed.
It is God who gives bread to the hungry,
the Lord, who sets prisoners free,

the Lord who gives sight to the blind,
who raises up those who are bowed down,
the Lord, who protects the stranger
and upholds the widow and orphan.

It is the Lord who loves the just
but thwarts the path of the wicked.
The Lord will reign for ever,
Zion's God, from age to age.

Alleluia!

Through the Year: Romans 12:1–2

I appeal to you, brothers and sisters, by the mercies of God, to present your bodies as a living sacrifice, holy and acceptable to God, which is your spiritual worship. Do not be conformed to this world, but be transformed by the renewing of your minds, so that you may discern what is the will of God – what is good and acceptable and perfect.

Joyful Hope: Jeremiah 30:21–22

Their prince shall be one of their own, their ruler shall come from their midst; I will bring him near, and he shall approach me, for who would otherwise dare to approach me? says the Lord. And you shall be my people, and I will be your God.

Word Made Flesh: 2 Timothy 1:9–10

God saved us and called us with a holy calling, not according to our works but according to his own purpose and grace. This grace was given to us in Christ Jesus before the ages began, but it has now been revealed through the appearing of our Saviour Christ Jesus, who abolished death and brought life and immortality to light through the gospel.

Penitence: 1 Corinthians 9:24–25

Do you not know that in a race the runners all compete, but only one receives the prize? Run in such a way that you may win it. Athletes exercise self-control in all things; they do it to receive a perishable garland, but we an imperishable one.

Resurrection and New Life: Luke 24:46–49

Jesus said to the disciples, 'Thus it is written, that the Messiah is to suffer and to rise from the dead on the third day, and that repentance and forgiveness of sins is to be proclaimed in his name to all nations, beginning from Jerusalem. You are witnesses of these things. And see, I am sending upon you what my Father promised; so stay here in the city until you have been clothed with power from on high.'

WEDNESDAY EVENING

Psalm 130

Out of the depths I cry to you, O Lord,
Lord, hear my voice!
O let your ears be attentive
to the voice of my pleading.

If you, O Lord, should mark our guilt,
Lord, who would survive?
But with you is found forgiveness:
for this we revere you.

My soul is waiting for the Lord.
I count on God's word.
My soul is longing for the Lord
more than those who watch for daybreak.
Let the watchers count on daybreak
and Israel on the Lord.

Because with the Lord there is mercy
and fullness of redemption,
Israel indeed God will redeem
from all its iniquity.

The Scripture Reading from the selection on the facing page.

Responsory (from Psalm 31:5, 6)

V.   You are my shelter; I put myself in your hands.
R.   **You are my shelter; I put myself in your hands.**
V.   Knowing you will save me, Lord God of truth,
R.   **I put myself in your hands.**
V.   Glory to the Father, the Son, the Holy Spirit.
R.   **You are my shelter; I put myself in your hands.**

Prayer in the Evening concludes on page 167.
Prayer in the Evening concludes on page 167.

Through the Year: Ephesians 4:25–27
Putting away falsehood, let all of us speak the truth to our neighbours, for we are members of one another. Be angry but do not sin; do not let the sun go down on your anger, and do not make room for the devil.

Joyful Hope: 1 Corinthians 4:5
Do not pronounce judgement before the time, before the Lord comes, who will bring to light the things now hidden in darkness and will disclose the purposes of the heart. Then each one will receive commendation from God.

Word Made Flesh: Galatians 4:4–5
When the fullness of time had come, God sent his Son, born of a woman, born under the law, in order to redeem those who were under the law, so that we might receive adoption as children.

Penitence: Isaiah 53:11–12
Out of his anguish he shall see light; he shall find satisfaction through his knowledge. The righteous one, my servant, shall make many righteous, and he shall bear their iniquities. Therefore I will allot him a portion with the great, and he shall divide the spoil with the strong; because he poured out himself to death, and was numbered with the transgressors; yet he bore the sin of many, and made intercession for the transgressors.

Passion: Ephesians 4:32–5:2
Be kind to one another, tender-hearted, forgiving one another, as God in Christ has forgiven you. Therefore be imitators of God, as beloved children, and live in love, as Christ loved us and gave himself up for us, a fragrant offering and sacrifice to God.

Resurrection and New Life: 1 Peter 2:4–5
Come to him, a living stone, though rejected by mortals yet chosen and precious in God's sight, and like living stones, let yourselves be built into a spiritual house, to be a holy priesthood, to offer spiritual sacrifices acceptable to God through Jesus Christ.

THURSDAY MORNING

Psalm 67

> O God, be gracious and bless us
> and let your face shed its light upon us.
> So will your ways be known upon earth
> and all nations learn your saving help.
>
> Let the peoples praise you, O God;
> let all the peoples praise you.
>
> Let the nations be glad and exult
> for you rule the world with justice.
> With fairness you rule the peoples,
> you guide the nations on earth.
>
> Let the peoples praise you, O God;
> let all the peoples praise you.
>
> The earth has yielded its fruit
> for God, our God, has blessed us.
> May God still give us blessing
> till the ends of the earth stand in awe.
>
> Let the peoples praise you, O God;
> let all the peoples praise you.

The Scripture Reading from the selection on the facing page.

Responsory (from Psalm 103:8)

> V.   The Lord is tender and caring.
> R.   **The Lord is tender and caring.**
> V.   Slow to anger, rich in love,
> R.   **tender and caring.**
> V.   Glory to the Father, the Son, the Holy Spirit.
> R.   **The Lord is tender and caring.**

Prayer in the Morning concludes on page 166.

Through the Year: John 13:34–35

I give you a new commandment, that you love one another. Just as I have loved you, you also should love one another. By this everyone will know that you are my disciples, if you have love for one another.

Joyful Hope: 1 Thessalonians 5:23–24

May the God of peace himself sanctify you entirely; and may your spirit and soul and body be kept sound and blameless at the coming of our Lord Jesus Christ. The one who calls you is faithful, and he will do this.

Word Made Flesh: John 1:1–5

In the beginning was the Word, and the Word was with God, and the Word was God. He was in the beginning with God. All things came into being through him, and without him not one thing came into being. What has come into being in him was life, and the life was the light of all people. The light shines in the darkness, and the darkness did not overcome it.

Penitence: Romans 5:8–9

God proves his love for us in that while we still were sinners Christ died for us. Much more surely then, now that we have been justified by his blood, will we be saved through him from the wrath of God.

Maundy Thursday: Hebrews 13:12–13

Jesus suffered outside the city gate in order to sanctify the people by his own blood. Let us then go to him outside the camp and bear the abuse he endured.

Resurrection and New Life: Matthew 28:18–20

All authority in heaven and on earth has been given to me. Go therefore and make disciples of all nations, baptizing them in the name of the Father and of the Son and of the Holy Spirit, and teaching them to obey everything that I have commanded you. And remember, I am with you always, to the end of the age.

Ascension Day: Hebrews 10:12–14

When Christ had offered for all time a single sacrifice for sins, he sat down at the right hand of God, and since then has been waiting until his enemies would be made a footstool for his feet. For by a single offering he has perfected for all time those who are sanctified.

THURSDAY DURING THE DAY

Psalm 46

God is for us a refuge and strength,
a helper close at hand, in time of distress,
so we shall not fear though the earth should rock,
though the mountains fall into the depths of the sea;
even though its waters rage and foam,
even though the mountains be shaken by its waves.

The Lord of hosts is with us;
the God of Jacob is our stronghold.

The waters of a river give joy to God's city,
the holy place where the Most High dwells.
God is within, it cannot be shaken;
God will help it at the dawning of the day.
Nations are in tumult, kingdoms are shaken;
God's voice roars forth, the earth shrinks away.

The Lord of hosts is with us;
the God of Jacob is our stronghold.

Come, consider the works of the Lord,
the redoubtable deeds God has done on the earth:
putting an end to wars across the earth;
breaking the bow, snapping the spear;
burning the shields with fire.
'Be still and know that I am God,
supreme among the nations, supreme on the earth!'

The Lord of hosts is with us;
the God of Jacob is our stronghold.

Through the Year: Galatians 5:16, 22–23a, 25

Live by the Spirit, I say, and do not gratify the desires of the flesh. The fruit of the Spirit is love, joy, peace, patience, kindness, generosity, faithfulness, gentleness, and self-control. If we live by the Spirit, let us also be guided by the Spirit.

Joyful Hope: 1 Thessalonians 3:12–13

May the Lord make you increase and abound in love for one another and for all, just as we abound in love for you. And may he so strengthen your hearts in holiness that you may be blameless before our God and Father at the coming of our Lord Jesus with all his saints.

Word Made Flesh: Titus 3:4–6

When the goodness and loving-kindness of God our Saviour appeared, he saved us, not because of any works of righteousness that we had done, but according to his mercy, through the water of rebirth and renewal by the Holy Spirit. This Spirit he poured out on us richly through Jesus Christ our Saviour.

Penitence: James 5:16, 19–20

Confess your sins to one another, and pray for one another, so that you may be healed. The prayer of the righteous is powerful and effective. My brothers and sisters, if anyone among you wanders from the truth and is brought back by another, you should know that whoever brings back a sinner from wandering will save the sinner's soul from death and will cover a multitude of sins.

Resurrection and New Life: Acts 2:42–45

The believers devoted themselves to the apostles' teaching and fellowship, to the breaking of bread and the prayers. Awe came upon everyone, because many wonders and signs were being done by the apostles. All who believed were together and had all things in common; they would sell their possessions and goods and distribute the proceeds to all, as any had need.

Ascension Day: John 16:33

Jesus said, 'In me you may have peace. In the world you face persecution. But take courage; I have conquered the world!'

THURSDAY EVENING

Psalm 23

> Lord, you are my shepherd;
> there is nothing I shall want.
> Fresh and green are the pastures
> where you give me repose.
> Near restful waters you lead me,
> to revive my drooping spirit.
>
> You guide me along the right path;
> you are true to your name.
> If I should walk in the valley of darkness
> no evil would I fear.
> You are there with your crook and your staff;
> with these you give me comfort.
>
> You have prepared a banquet for me
> in the sight of my foes.
> My head you have anointed with oil;
> my cup is overflowing.
>
> Surely goodness and kindness shall follow me
> all the days of my life.
> In the Lord's own house shall I dwell
> for ever and ever.

The Scripture Reading from the selection on the facing page.

Responsory (from Psalm 90:16, 17)

> V. Let your servants see the splendour of your work.
> R. **Let your servants see the splendour of your work.**
> V. Let your loveliness shine on us,
> R. **the splendour of your work.**
> V. Glory to the Father, the Son, the Holy Spirit.
> R. **Let your servants see the splendour of your work.**

Prayer in the Evening concludes on page 167.

Through the Year: Mark 10:43–45

Whoever wishes to become great among you must be your servant, and whoever wishes to be first among you must be slave of all. For the Son of Man came not to be served but to serve, and to give his life a ransom for many.

Joyful Hope: Micah 5:4–5a

He shall stand and feed his flock in the strength of the Lord, in the majesty of the name of the Lord his God. And they shall live secure, for now he shall be great to the ends of the earth; and he shall be the one of peace.

Word Made Flesh: 1 John 4:14–15

We have seen and do testify that the Father has sent his Son as the Saviour of the world. God abides in those who confess that Jesus is the Son of God, and they abide in God.

Penitence: John 3:16–17

God so loved the world that he gave his only Son, so that everyone who believes in him may not perish but may have eternal life. Indeed, God did not send the Son into the world to condemn the world, but in order that the world might be saved through him.

Maundy Thursday: Matthew 26:31–32

Jesus said to them, 'You will all become deserters because of me this night; for it is written, "I will strike the shepherd, and the sheep of the flock will be scattered." But after I am raised up, I will go ahead of you to Galilee.'

Resurrection and New Life: John 14:26–27

The Advocate, the Holy Spirit, whom the Father will send in my name, will teach you everything, and remind you of all that I have said to you. Peace I leave with you; my peace I give to you. I do not give to you as the world gives. Do not let your hearts be troubled, and do not let them be afraid.

Ascension Day: Mark 16:19–20

The Lord Jesus, after he had spoken to them, was taken up into heaven and sat down at the right hand of God. And they went out and proclaimed the good news every-where, while the Lord worked with them and confirmed the message by the signs that accompanied it.

FRIDAY MORNING

Psalm 85

O Lord, you once favoured your land
and revived the fortunes of Jacob,
you forgave the guilt of your people
and covered all their sins.
You averted all your rage,
you calmed the heat of your anger.

Revive us now, God, our helper!
Put an end to your grievance against us.
Will you be angry with us for ever,
will your anger never cease?

Will you not restore again our life
that your people may rejoice in you?
Let us see, O Lord, your mercy
and give us your saving help.

I will hear what the Lord has to say,
a voice that speaks of peace,
peace for his people and friends
and those who turn to God in their hearts.
Salvation is near for the God-fearing,
and his glory will dwell in our land.

Mercy and faithfulness have met;
justice and peace have embraced.
Faithfulness shall spring from the earth
and justice look down from heaven.

The Lord will make us prosper
and our earth shall yield its fruit.
Justice shall march in the forefront,
and peace shall follow the way.

The Scripture Reading from the selection on the facing page.

Responsory (from Psalm 145:8, 9)

    V.   Gracious and merciful is the Lord, slow to anger, full of love.
    R.   **Gracious and merciful is the Lord, slow to anger, full of love.**
    V.   The Lord is good in every way,
    R.   **slow to anger, full of love.**
    V.   Glory to the Father, the Son, the Holy Spirit.
    R.   **Gracious and merciful is the Lord, slow to anger, full of love.**

Prayer in the Morning concludes on page 166.

Through the Year: Romans 8:18–21

I consider that the sufferings of this present time are not worth comparing with the glory about to be revealed to us. For the creation waits with eager longing for the revealing of the children of God; for the creation was subjected to futility, not of its own will but by the will of the one who subjected it, in hope that the creation itself will be set free from its bondage to decay and will obtain the freedom of the glory of the children of God.

Joyful Hope: Romans 13:11–12

You know what time it is, how it is now the moment for you to wake from sleep. For salvation is nearer to us now than when we became believers; the night is far gone, the day is near. Let us then lay aside the works of darkness and put on the armour of light.

Word Made Flesh: Isaiah 11:1–2

A shoot shall come out from the stump of Jesse, and a branch shall grow out of his roots. The spirit of the Lord shall rest on him, the spirit of wisdom and understanding, the spirit of counsel and might, the spirit of knowledge and the fear of the Lord.

Penitence: Luke 9:23–24

Jesus said to them all, 'If any want to become my followers, let them deny themselves and take up their cross daily and follow me. For those who want to save their life will lose it, and those who lose their life for my sake will save it.'

Good Friday: 1 Peter 2:21–24

Christ suffered for you, leaving you an example, so that you should follow in his steps. He committed no sin, and no deceit was found in his mouth. When he was abused, he did not return abuse; when he suffered, he did not threaten; but he entrusted himself to the one who judges justly. He himself bore our sins in his body on the cross, so that, free from sins, we might live for righteousness; by his wounds you have been healed.

Resurrection and New Life: Acts 5:30–32

The God of our ancestors raised up Jesus, whom you had killed by hanging him on a tree. God exalted him at his right hand as Leader and Saviour, so that he might give repentance to Israel and forgiveness of sins. And we are witnesses to these things, and so is the Holy Spirit whom God has given to those who obey him.

FRIDAY DURING THE DAY

Psalm 57

Have mercy on me, God, have mercy
for in you my soul has taken refuge.
In the shadow of your wings I take refuge
till the storms of destruction pass by.

I call to you God the Most High,
to you who have always been my help.
May you send from heaven and save me
and shame those who assail me.

O God, send your truth and your love.

My soul lies down among lions,
who would devour us, one and all.
Their teeth are spears and arrows,
their tongue a sharpened sword.

O God, arise above the heavens;
may your glory shine on earth!

They laid a snare for my steps,
my soul was bowed down.
They dug a pit in my path
but fell in it themselves.

My heart is ready, O God,
my heart is ready.
I will sing, I will sing your praise.
Awake, my soul;
awake, lyre and harp,
I will awake the dawn.

I will thank you, Lord, among the peoples,
among the nations I will praise you
for your love reaches to the heavens
and your truth to the skies.

O God, arise above the heavens;
may your glory shine on earth!

Through the Year: Romans 8:14–17

All who are led by the Spirit of God are children of God. For you did not receive a spirit of slavery to fall back into fear, but you have received a spirit of adoption. When we cry, 'Abba! Father!' it is that very Spirit bearing witness with our spirit that we are children of God, and if children, then heirs, heirs of God and joint heirs with Christ – if, in fact, we suffer with him so that we may also be glorified with him.

Joyful Hope: James 5:7–9

Be patient, beloved, until the coming of the Lord. The farmer waits for the precious crop from the earth, being patient with it until it receives the early and the late rains. You also must be patient. Strengthen your hearts, for the coming of the Lord is near. Beloved, do not grumble against one another, so that you may not be judged. See, the Judge is standing at the doors!

Word Made Flesh: Luke 2:34–35

Simeon blessed them and said to Mary, 'This child is destined for the falling and the rising of many in Israel, and to be a sign that will be opposed so that the inner thoughts of many will be revealed – and a sword will pierce your own soul too.'

Penitence: 1 Corinthians 1:18

The message about the cross is foolishness to those who are perishing, but to us who are being saved it is the power of God.

Resurrection and New Life: Acts 2:22b–24

Jesus of Nazareth, a man attested to you by God with deeds of power, wonders, and signs that God did through him among you, as you yourselves know – this man, handed over to you according to the definite plan and foreknowledge of God, you crucified and killed by the hands of those outside the law. But God raised him up, having freed him from death, because it was impossible for him to be held in its power.

FRIDAY EVENING

Psalm 90:1–9, 11–12, 14

O Lord, you have been our refuge
from one generation to the next.
Before the mountains were born
or the earth or the world brought forth,
you are God, without beginning or end.

You turn us back into dust
and say: 'Go back, children of the earth.'
To your eyes a thousand years
are like yesterday, come and gone,
no more than a watch in the night.

You sweep us away like a dream,
like grass which springs up in the morning.
In the morning it springs up and flowers;
by evening it withers and fades.

So we are destroyed in your anger,
struck with terror in your fury.
Our guilt lies open before you,
our secrets in the light of your face.

All our days pass away in your anger.
Our life is over like a sigh.
Who understands the power of your anger
and fears the strength of your fury?

Make us know the shortness of our life
that we may gain wisdom of heart.
In the morning, fill us with your love;
we shall exult and rejoice all our days.

The Scripture Reading from the selection on the facing page.

Responsory (from Psalm 141:1, 2)

V.   Lord, I call and call. Listen when I plead with you.
R.   **Lord, I call and call. Listen when I plead with you.**
V.   Let my prayer rise like an evening sacrifice.
R.   **Listen when I plead with you.**
V.   Glory to the Father, the Son, the Holy Spirit.
R.   **Lord, I call and call. Listen when I plead with you.**

Prayer in the Evening concludes on page 167.

Through the Year: Matthew 11:28–30

Come to me, all you that are weary and are carrying heavy burdens, and I will give you rest. Take my yoke upon you, and learn from me; for I am gentle and humble in heart, and you will find rest for your souls. For my yoke is easy, and my burden is light.

Joyful Hope: 1 Thessalonians 5:4–5, 8–10

You, beloved, are not in darkness, for that day to surprise you like a thief; for you are all children of light and children of the day; we are not of the night or of darkness. But since we belong to the day, let us be sober, and put on the breastplate of faith and love, and for a helmet the hope of salvation. For God has destined us not for wrath but for obtaining salvation through our Lord Jesus Christ, who died for us, so that whether we are awake or asleep we may live with him.

Word Made Flesh: Philippians 2:5–7

Let the same mind be in you that was in Christ Jesus, who, though he was in the form of God, did not regard equality with God as something to be exploited, but emptied himself, taking the form of a slave, being born in human likeness.

Penitence: John 12:24–25

Very truly, I tell you, unless a grain of wheat falls into the earth and dies, it remains just a single grain; but if it dies, it bears much fruit. Those who love their life lose it, and those who hate their life in this world will keep it for eternal life.

Good Friday: Zechariah 12:10

I will pour out a spirit of compassion and supplication on the house of David and the inhabitants of Jerusalem, so that, when they look on the one whom they have pierced, they shall mourn for him, as one mourns for an only child, and weep bitterly over him, as one weeps over a firstborn.

Resurrection and New Life: Romans 8:10–11

If Christ is in you, though the body is dead because of sin, the Spirit is life because of righteousness. If the Spirit of him who raised Jesus from the dead dwells in you, he who raised Christ from the dead will give life to your mortal bodies also through his Spirit that dwells in you.

SATURDAY MORNING

Psalm 121

> I lift up my eyes to the mountains;
> from where shall come my help?
> My help shall come from the Lord
> who made heaven and earth.
>
> May God never allow you to stumble!
> Let your guard not sleep.
> Behold, neither sleeping nor slumbering,
> Israel's guard.
>
> The Lord is your guard and your shade;
> and stands at your right.
> By day the sun shall not smite you
> nor the moon in the night.
>
> The Lord will guard you from evil,
> and will guard your soul.
> The Lord will guard your going and coming
> both now and for ever.

The Scripture Reading from the selection on the facing page.

Responsory (from Psalm 145:10, 11)

> V. Let your works praise you, Lord, let them tell of your might.
> R. **Let your works praise you, Lord, let them tell of your might.**
> V. Let them proclaim your glorious reign,
> R. **let them tell of your might.**
> V. Glory to the Father, the Son, the Holy Spirit.
> R. **Let your works praise you, Lord, let them tell of your might.**

Prayer in the Morning concludes on page 166.

Through the Year: Colossians 3:16–17

Let the word of Christ dwell in you richly; teach and admonish one another in all wisdom; and with gratitude in your hearts sing psalms, hymns, and spiritual songs to God. And whatever you do, in word or deed, do everything in the name of the Lord Jesus, giving thanks to God the Father through him.

Joyful Hope: Isaiah 2:3

Many peoples shall come and say, 'Come, let us go up to the mountain of the Lord, to the house of the God of Jacob; that he may teach us his ways and that we may walk in his paths.' For out of Zion shall go forth instruction, and the word of the Lord from Jerusalem.

Word Made Flesh: Matthew 1:22–23

All this took place to fulfil what had been spoken by the Lord through the prophet: 'Look, the virgin shall conceive and bear a son, and they shall name him Emmanuel,' which means, 'God is with us.'

Penitence: Romans 12:1–2

I appeal to you, brothers and sisters, by the mercies of God, to present your bodies as a living sacrifice, holy and acceptable to God, which is your spiritual worship. Do not be conformed to this world, but be transformed by the renewing of your minds, so that you may discern what is the will of God – what is good and acceptable and perfect.

Holy Saturday: Romans 6:2–4

How can we who died to sin go on living in it? Do you not know that all of us who have been baptized into Christ Jesus were baptized into his death? Therefore we have been buried with him by baptism into death, so that, just as Christ was raised from the dead by the glory of the Father, so we too might walk in newness of life.

Resurrection and New Life: John 11:25–26

Jesus said, 'I am the resurrection and the life. Those who believe in me, even though they die, will live, and everyone who lives and believes in me will never die.'

SATURDAY DURING THE DAY

Psalm 65

To you our praise is due
in Zion, O God.
To you we pay our vows,
you who hear our prayer.

To you all flesh will come
with its burden of sin.
Too heavy for us, our offences,
but you wipe them away.

Blessed those whom you choose and call
to dwell in your courts.
We are filled with the blessings of your house,
of your holy temple.

You keep your pledge with wonders,
O God our saviour,
the hope of all the earth
and of far distant isles.

You uphold the mountains with your strength,
you are girded with power.
You still the roaring of the seas,
the roaring of their waves,
and the tumult of the peoples.

The ends of the earth stand in awe
at the sight of your wonders.
The lands of sunrise and sunset
you fill with your joy.

You care for the earth, give it water;
you fill it with riches.
Your river in heaven brims over
to provide its grain.

And thus you provide for the earth;
you drench its furrows;
you level it, soften it with showers;
you bless its growth.

You crown the year with your goodness.
Abundance flows in your steps;
in the pastures of the wilderness it flows.

The hills are girded with joy,
the meadows covered with flocks,
the valleys are decked with wheat.
They shout for joy, yes, they sing.

Through the Year: Matthew 22:37–40

Jesus said, '"You shall love the Lord your God with all your heart, and with all your soul, and with all your mind." This is the greatest and first commandment. And a second is like it: "You shall love your neighbour as yourself." On these two commandments hang all the law and the prophets.'

Joyful Hope: Philippians 3:20–21

Our citizenship is in heaven, and it is from there that we are expecting a Saviour, the Lord Jesus Christ. He will transform the body of our humiliation so that it may be conformed to the body of his glory, by the power that also enables him to make all things subject to himself.

Word Made Flesh: Luke 1:35

The angel said to Mary, 'The Holy Spirit will come upon you, and the power of the Most High will overshadow you; therefore the child to be born will be holy; he will be called Son of God.'

Penitence: Nehemiah 8:10

Go your way, eat the fat and drink sweet wine and send portions of them to those for whom nothing is prepared, for this day is holy to our Lord; and do not be grieved, for the joy of the Lord is your strength.

Resurrection and New Life: 1 Peter 2:9–10

You are a chosen race, a royal priesthood, a holy nation, God's own people, in order that you may proclaim the mighty acts of him who called you out of darkness into his marvellous light. Once you were not a people, but now you are God's people; once you had not received mercy, but now you have received mercy.

SATURDAY EVENING

Psalm 134

> O come, bless the Lord,
> all you who serve the Lord,
> who stand in the house of the Lord,
> in the courts of the house of our God.
>
> Lift up your hands to the holy place
> and bless the Lord through the night.
>
> May the Lord bless you from Zion,
> God who made both heaven and earth.

The Scripture Reading from the selection on the facing page.

Responsory (Traditional)

V.   Save us, Lord, while we are awake, protect us while we sleep.
R.   **Save us, Lord, while we are awake, protect us while we sleep.**
V.   May we keep watch with Christ, and rest with him in peace.
R.   **Protect us while we sleep.**
V.   Glory to the Father, the Son, the Holy Spirit.
R.   **Save us, Lord, while we are awake, protect us while we sleep.**

Prayer in the Evening concludes on page 167.

Through the Year: Isaiah 30:15

For thus said the Lord God, the Holy One of Israel: In returning and rest you shall be saved; in quietness and in trust shall be your strength.

Joyful Hope: 2 Peter 3:8–9

Do not ignore this one fact, beloved, that with the Lord one day is like a thousand years, and a thousand years are like one day. The Lord is not slow about his promise, as some think of slowness, but is patient with you, not wanting any to perish, but all to come to repentance.

Word Made Flesh: 1 Peter 5:5b–7

All of you must clothe yourselves with humility in your dealings with one another, for 'God opposes the proud, but gives grace to the humble.' Humble yourselves therefore under the mighty hand of God, so that he may exalt you in due time. Cast all your anxiety on him, because he cares for you.

Penitence: James 4:7–8, 10

Submit yourselves to God. Resist the devil, and he will flee from you. Draw near to God, and he will draw near to you. Cleanse your hands, you sinners, and purify your hearts, you double-minded. Humble yourselves before the Lord, and he will exalt you.

Holy Saturday: Hebrews 4:9–11

A sabbath rest still remains for the people of God; for those who enter God's rest also cease from their labours as God did from his. Let us therefore make every effort to enter that rest, so that no one may fall through such disobedience as theirs.

Resurrection and New Life: Romans 14:7–9

We do not live to ourselves, and we do not die to ourselves. If we live, we live to the Lord, and if we die, we die to the Lord; so then, whether we live or whether we die, we are the Lord's. For to this end Christ died and lived again, so that he might be Lord of both the dead and the living.

SAINTS' AND HOLY DAYS – MORNING

Psalm 92

> It is good to give thanks to the Lord,
> to make music to your name, O Most High,
> to proclaim your love in the morning
> and your truth in the watches of the night,
> on the ten-stringed lyre and the lute,
> with the murmuring sound of the harp.
>
> Your deeds, O Lord, have made me glad;
> for the work of your hands I shout with joy.
> O Lord, how great are your works!
> How deep are your designs!
> The stupid cannot know this
> and the foolish cannot understand.
>
> Though the wicked spring up like grass
> and all who do evil thrive,
> they are doomed to be eternally destroyed.
> But you, Lord, are eternally on high.
> See how your enemies perish;
> all doers of evil are scattered.
>
> To me you give the wild ox's strength;
> you anoint me with the purest oil.
> My eyes looked in triumph on my foes;
> my ears heard gladly of their fall.
> The just will flourish like the palm tree
> and grow like a Lebanon cedar.
>
> Planted in the house of the Lord
> they will flourish in the courts of our God,
> still bearing fruit when they are old,
> still full of sap, still green,
> to proclaim that the Lord is just.
> My rock, in whom there is no wrong.

The Scripture Reading from the selection on the facing page.

The Responsory (from Psalm 32:11)

> V.   Rejoice in the Lord, let the just shout for joy.
> R.   **Rejoice in the Lord, let the just shout for joy.**
> V.   Let the upright sing praise,
> R.   **let the just shout for joy.**
> V.   Glory to the Father, the Son, the Holy Spirit.
> R.   **Rejoice in the Lord, let the just shout for joy.**

Prayer in the Morning concludes on page 166.

Feasts of Our Lord: Romans 8:16–17

It is that very Spirit bearing witness with our spirit that we are children of God, and if children, then heirs, heirs of God and joint heirs with Christ – if, in fact, we suffer with him so that we may also be glorified with him.

Apostles and Evangelists: Acts 2:42–45

The believers devoted themselves to the apostles' teaching and fellowship, to the breaking of bread and the prayers. Awe came upon everyone, because many wonders and signs were being done by the apostles. All who believed were together and had all things in common; they would sell their possessions and goods and distribute the proceeds to all, as any had need.

Mary: Galatians 4:4–5

When the fullness of time had come, God sent his Son, born of a woman, born under the law, in order to redeem those who were under the law, so that we might receive adoption as children.

Martyrs: Romans 8:35, 37–39

Who will separate us from the love of Christ? Will hardship, or distress, or persecution, or famine, or nakedness, or peril, or sword? No, in all these things we are more than conquerors through him who loved us. For I am convinced that neither death, nor life, nor angels, nor rulers, nor things present, nor things to come, nor powers, nor height, nor depth, nor anything else in all creation, will be able to separate us from the love of God in Christ Jesus our Lord.

Pastors: 1 Peter 5:1–4

As an elder myself and a witness of the sufferings of Christ, as well as one who shares in the glory to be revealed, I exhort the elders among you to tend the flock of God that is in your charge, exercising the oversight, not under compulsion but willingly, as God would have you do it – not for sordid gain but eagerly. Do not lord it over those in your charge, but be examples to the flock. And when the chief shepherd appears, you will win the crown of glory that never fades away.

Others: Revelation 7:15–17

They are before the throne of God, and worship him day and night within his temple, and the one who is seated on the throne will shelter them. They will hunger no more, and thirst no more; the sun will not strike them, nor any scorching heat; for the Lamb at the centre of the throne will be their shepherd, and he will guide them to springs of the water of life, and God will wipe away every tear from their eyes.

SAINTS' AND HOLY DAYS – DURING THE DAY

Psalm 148 ('Alleluia!' is omitted in Lent)

> Alleluia!
>
> Praise the Lord from the heavens,
> praise God in the heights.
> Praise God, all you angels,
> praise him, all you host.
>
> Praise God, sun and moon,
> praise him, shining stars.
> Praise God, highest heavens
> and the waters above the heavens.
>
> Let them praise the name of the Lord.
> The Lord commanded: they were made.
> God fixed them for ever,
> gave a law which shall not pass away.
>
> Praise the Lord from the earth,
> sea creatures and all oceans,
> fire and hail, snow and mist,
> stormy winds that obey God's word;
>
> all mountains and hills,
> all fruit trees and cedars,
> beasts, wild and tame,
> reptiles and birds on the wing;
>
> all earth's nations and peoples,
> earth's leaders and rulers;
> young men and maidens,
> the old together with children.
>
> Let them praise the name of the Lord
> who alone is exalted.
> The splendour of God's name
> reaches beyond heaven and earth.
>
> God exalts the strength of the people,
> is the praise of all the saints,
> of the sons and daughters of Israel,
> of the people to whom he comes close.
>
> Alleluia!

The Scripture Reading from the selection on the facing page.

Feasts of Our Lord: Revelation 21:10–11, 23

In the spirit the angel carried me away to a great, high mountain and showed me the holy city Jerusalem coming down out of heaven from God. It has the glory of God and a radiance like a very rare jewel, like jasper, clear as crystal. And the city has no need of sun or moon to shine on it, for the glory of God is its light, and its lamp is the Lamb.

Apostles and Evangelists: Ephesians 4:11–13

The gifts Christ gave were that some would be apostles, some prophets, some evangelists, some pastors and teachers, to equip the saints for the work of ministry, for building up the body of Christ, until all of us come to the unity of the faith and of the knowledge of the Son of God, to maturity, to the measure of the full stature of Christ.

Mary: Isaiah 61:10

I will greatly rejoice in the Lord, my whole being shall exult in my God; for he has clothed me with the garments of salvation, he has covered me with the robe of righteousness, as a bridegroom decks himself with a garland, and as a bride adorns herself with her jewels.

Martyrs: Matthew 5:10–12

Blessed are those who are persecuted for righteousness' sake, for theirs is the kingdom of heaven. Blessed are you when people revile you and persecute you and utter all kinds of evil against you falsely on my account. Rejoice and be glad, for your reward is great in heaven, for in the same way they persecuted the prophets who were before you.

Pastors: Philippians 3:7–8a

Whatever gains I had, these I have come to regard as loss because of Christ. More than that, I regard everything as loss because of the surpassing value of knowing Christ Jesus my Lord.

Others: Revelation 21:2–3, 22, 27

I saw the holy city, the new Jerusalem, coming down out of heaven from God, prepared as a bride adorned for her husband. And I heard a loud voice from the throne saying, 'See, the home of God is among mortals. He will dwell with them; they will be his peoples, and God himself will be with them.' I saw no temple in the city, for its temple is the Lord God the Almighty and the Lamb. But nothing unclean will enter it, nor anyone who practises abomination or falsehood, but only those who are written in the Lamb's book of life.

SAINTS' AND HOLY DAYS – EVENING

Psalm 139:1–12,17–18

O Lord, you search me and you know me,
you know my resting and my rising,
you discern my purpose from afar.
You mark when I walk or lie down,
all my ways lie open to you.

Before ever a word is on my tongue
you know it, O Lord, through and through.
Behind and before you besiege me,
your hand ever laid upon me.
Too wonderful for me, this knowledge,
too high, beyond my reach.

O where can I go from your spirit,
or where can I flee from your face?
If I climb the heavens, you are there.
If I lie in the grave, you are there.

If I take the wings of the dawn
and dwell at the sea's furthest end,
even there your hand would lead me,
your right hand would hold me fast.

If I say: 'Let the darkness hide me
and the light around me be night,'
even darkness is not dark for you
and the night is as clear as the day.

To me, how mysterious your thoughts,
the sum of them not to be numbered!
If I count them, they are more than the sand;
to finish, I must be eternal, like you.

The Scripture Reading from the selection on the facing page.

The Responsory (from Psalm 103:3–5)

V.   Bless God, who enfolds you with tender care.
R.   **Bless God, who enfolds you with tender care.**
V.   Who gives you an eagle's strength,
R.   **who enfolds you with tender care.**
V.   Glory to the Father, the Son, the Holy Spirit.
R.   **Bless God, who enfolds you with tender care.**

Prayer in the Evening concludes on page 167.

Feasts of Our Lord: Philippians 3:20–21

Our citizenship is in heaven, and it is from there that we are expecting a Saviour, the Lord Jesus Christ. He will transform the body of our humiliation so that it may be conformed to the body of his glory, by the power that also enables him to make all things subject to himself.

Apostles and Evangelists: Ephesians 2:19–22

You are no longer strangers and aliens, but you are citizens with the saints and also members of the household of God, built upon the foundation of the apostles and prophets, with Christ Jesus himself as the cornerstone. In him the whole structure is joined together and grows into a holy temple in the Lord; in whom you also are built together spiritually into a dwelling-place for God.

Mary: Luke 1:38

Mary said, 'Here am I, the servant of the Lord; let it be with me according to your word.'

Martyrs: 1 Peter 4:13–14

Rejoice in so far as you are sharing Christ's sufferings, so that you may also be glad and shout for joy when his glory is revealed. If you are reviled for the name of Christ, you are blessed, because the spirit of glory, which is the Spirit of God, is resting on you.

Pastors: Hebrews 13:7–9a

Remember your leaders, those who spoke the word of God to you; consider the outcome of their way of life, and imitate their faith. Jesus Christ is the same yesterday and today and for ever. Do not be carried away by all kinds of strange teachings; for it is well for the heart to be strengthened by grace.

Others: Hebrews 12:22–24

You have come to Mount Zion and to the city of the living God, the heavenly Jerusalem, and to innumerable angels in festal gathering, and to the assembly of the firstborn who are enrolled in heaven, and to God the judge of all, and to the spirits of the righteous made perfect, and to Jesus, the mediator of a new covenant, and to the sprinkled blood that speaks a better word than the blood of Abel.

EVERY MORNING

Canticle: A Song of Moses and of the Lamb (Revelation 15:3–4)

Great and wonderful are your deeds,
Lord God the Almighty.
Just and true are your ways,
O Ruler of the nations.

Who shall not revere you
and praise your name, O Lord?
For you alone are holy.

All nations shall come and worship in your presence
for your just dealings have been revealed.

To the One who sits on the throne and to the Lamb
be blessing and honour and glory and might, for ever and ever. Amen.

*Prayer and thanksgiving may be offered, including the Lord's Prayer. The collect of the day may
be said, and one or more of these Concluding Prayers:*

Eternal God and Father,
you create us by your power and redeem us by your love:
    guide and strengthen us by your Spirit,
        that we may give ourselves in love and service
        to one another and to you;
through Jesus Christ our Lord. **Amen.**

O God of love, true light and radiance of our world,
    shine into our hearts like the rising sun,
    and banish the darkness of sin and the mists of error.
May we, this day and all our life, walk without stumbling
    along the way which you have set before us;
    through your Son Jesus Christ our Lord. **Amen.**

God, kindle within our hearts today a flame of love
    for our neighbours, for our foes, for our friends,
    for the brave, for the cowardly, for the thoughtless.
O Son of the loveliest Mary, in all that we love may we serve you,
    from the lowliest thing that lives,
    to the name that is highest of all. **Amen.**

Open wide the windows of our spirits, O Lord,
    and fill us full of light.
Open wide the door of our hearts,
    that we may receive and entertain you
        with all our powers of adoration and love. **Amen.**

CONCLUSION

**May the God of peace be with us, to guide us and empower us to do his will;
in the name of Jesus the Lord. Amen.**

EVERY EVENING

Canticle: The Song of Simeon (Luke 2:29–32)

> Now, Lord, you let your servant go in peace:
> your word has been fulfilled.

> My own eyes have seen the salvation
> which you have prepared in the sight of every people:

> A light to reveal you to the nations
> and the glory of your people Israel.

> Give praise to the Father...

Prayer and thanksgiving may be offered, including the Lord's Prayer. The collect of the day may be said, and one or more of these Concluding Prayers:

> Visit our homes, we pray you, Lord:
>> drive far away from them all the snares of the evil one.
> May your holy angels stay there and guard us in peace,
>> and let your blessing be always upon us.
> Through Christ our Lord. **Amen.**

> Keep watch, dear Lord,
>> with those who work, or watch, or weep this night,
>> and give your angels charge over those who sleep.
> Tend the sick, Lord Christ; give rest to the weary,
>> bless the dying, soothe the suffering,
>> pity the afflicted, shield the joyous;
>>> and all for your love's sake. **Amen.**

> Bless to us, O God, the moon that is above us,
> the earth that is beneath us, the friends who are around us,
> your image deep within us, the rest which is before us. **Amen.**

> O Lord God, from whom we come,
>> in whom we are enfolded,
>> to whom we shall return:
> Bless us in our pilgrimage through life;
>> with the power of the Father protecting,
>>> with the love of Jesus indwelling,
>>>> and the light of the Spirit guiding,
> until we come to our ending, in life and love eternal. **Amen.**

CONCLUSION

Evening:

The Lord bless us, and keep us from all evil, and bring us to everlasting life. Amen.

Night:

The Lord grant us a quiet night and a perfect end. Amen.

Commentary

The shape and structure of Daily Prayer

The use of Hymns, Psalms and Canticles

The arrangement of Scripture readings

Conclusion

THE SHAPE OF DAILY PRAYER

What follows is a description of the order for *Daily Prayer* in each of its seasonal versions. The shorter forms have a similar shape but with some of the elements omitted.

PRAISE

Opening

A statement about God, which leads us to 'Come, let us worship'.

Invitatory

Nearly always a few verses from one of the psalms, inviting us to rejoice in God and adore him. A Trinitarian doxology, and, except in Lent, the Hebrew cry 'Alleluia!' set our prayer in the Christian tradition with its Jewish origins.

Hymn or Acclamation

Poetry celebrating our faith in Christ. This may be said or sung.

Opening Prayer

We complete the Praise part of *Daily Prayer* by blessing God and asking that our lives may reflect his will. Any extempore offering of praise should be brief.

The whole of this first part of *Daily Prayer* may be said standing if the setting for prayer lends itself to this. Now it is time to be seated, and settle into the more meditative part of the order.

REFLECTION

Psalmody

Among the 150 psalms is found every mood of human experience. As we pray the psalms, we bring the whole human condition to God: its joys and longings, its laments and thanksgivings.

Canticle of the Day

This forms a continuation of the psalmody, with a text from Scripture or from the Church's rich store, ancient or modern. The song celebrates God's goodness and our response in faith, hope and love.

Scripture Reading

Reading the Bible devotionally has a central place in Christian prayer. By doing this we get involved in the Bible's story as our own story, and sometimes we may hear a 'word of the Lord' for ourselves in it. Further spiritual reading, and/or silent reflection, may follow.

Responsory

This mulling over a verse or two of Scripture completes the reflection on the Word of God and sets that reflection in the context of the current season of the Christian year.

CANTICLE OF THE SEASON

This song is used daily through the course of a season and provides a focal point in *Daily Prayer*. As these songs focus on Christ, you may choose to make the sign of the cross during the opening words. It may be appropriate to stand to say or sing this canticle.

Following this song of praise, the mood of *Daily Prayer* turns to one of intercession and prayer. For this last section you may choose to remain standing, or you may prefer to sit or kneel.

PRAYER AND THANKSGIVING

The Lord's Prayer
The model of all Christian prayer, this unites us in prayer with our sisters and brothers everywhere and helps us get our priorities right for what follows. The 'modern version' printed on the loose card is the international, ecumenically agreed, English text without any adaptation, and we commend it to you. The optional introduction to this prayer is especially appropriate in communal use.

Intercessions and Thanksgivings
Here we provide no more than a framework and some suggestions. Each user or group will need to think through how they are going to approach this part of *Daily Prayer*, and which, if any, additional resources are to be used, such as a cycle of prayer. It is our privilege as the children of God to bring before him the needs of others as well as our own.

Responses
The responses, a different set in each season, give wings to the prayers we have just offered.

Collect
This prayer, which relates our daily prayer to the previous Sunday's corporate worship, should be used if it is available. Some churches print it on their weekly bulletin, and it can be found in many service books. The weekly collect is replaced on Saints' and Holy Days by one appropriate to the festival.

Concluding Prayer
Each season has a different set of four concluding prayers, which are drawn broadly from the following four categories: liturgical texts; prayers of the church fathers; Celtic, in origin or style; modern.

Conclusion
A brief sentence gives us assurance as we leave prayer and turn once more to the opportunities and demands of the day.

HYMN, PSALM, AND BIBLE READING

HYMN

A short chorus or acclamation is provided in each order of Daily Prayer, but if you have the resources available this could be replaced by a suitable hymn. We do encourage the use of a hymn or song, which can be spoken if singing seems inappropriate. All the acclamations we have included, along with their music, can be found in *Complete Anglican Hymns Old and New* (Kevin Mayhew Ltd). A good source of hymns in the style of the traditional 'Office Hymn' is *Hymns for Prayer and Praise* (Canterbury Press).

PSALM

The appointed psalm or psalms are indicated in the Lectionary Tables at the front of the book. The Psalms printed are from The Grail Translation (New Inclusive Language Version) and for consistency of style we recommend that you use this for the psalms set in the Lectionary (see page viii for details). You can of course choose whichever version of the psalms you prefer, but you should note that the verse numbering of different versions of the Psalter varies, so you may have to use your judgement on those occasions where a psalm is not used in full.

BIBLE READING

Each day's Scripture reading is found in the Lectionary Tables at the front of the book. The translation used is the New Revised Standard Version. You can of course use whichever translation of the Bible you prefer, but again there may be slight discrepancies in some of the references.

The way we give Bible references in the tables is shown by the following examples. Note that verse numbers are inclusive; read from the beginning of the first verse given to the end of the last verse given. Book titles are normally given in full at or near their first occurrence, but thereafter are usually abbreviated.

Gen. 4:1–16	Genesis. Chapter 4: from verse 1 to verse 16.
Mark 15:40–16:8	Mark. Chapter 15:
	from verse 40 to chapter 16: verse 8.

Most references are of these two sorts. Some are more complicated, as in the following examples:

2 Sam. 19:18b–43	The second Book of Samuel. Chapter 19:
	from the second half of verse 18 to verse 43.
Ezek. 1:1–12, 22–2:10	Ezekiel. Chapter 1: verses 1 to 12,
	then from verse 22 to chapter 2: verse 10.
1 Ki. 4:29–34; 6:1–14	The first Book of Kings. Chapter 4:
	verses 29 to 34; then chapter 6: verses 1 to 14.

A 'DAILY OFFICE'

Daily Prayer is in some ways radically new, yet at heart it is a version of something which is centuries old: the Church's tradition of daily, ordered prayer. This tradition was inherited from the synagogue: prayers and psalms, morning and evening, day by day, to sanctify the day to God. Over the centuries this tradition of prayer has been enriched and enlarged, particularly in the monastic movement. The Church of England, in common with the great historic Churches, has seen this 'Daily Office' as its spiritual heartbeat. While the clergy have normally been under obligation to pray in this way, large numbers of lay people have also shared in it at various times in the Church's history. The compilers believe that, given a form of Daily Office which is suited to the circumstances of most people's lives, large numbers of church members may again be drawn to participate in it. *Daily Prayer* is offered with that vision and hope.

ADAPTABILITY

This material is designed for use at any convenient time of the day, thus allowing for the hugely differing daily routines which people nowadays have. A resource for a one-, two-, or three-fold pattern of daily devotion.

SIMPLICITY, CONTINUITY, VARIETY

We have aimed to provide a resource for prayer which is reasonably straightforward to use; yet at the same time one which makes full use of the rich store of texts from the Scriptures and the long tradition of the Church. We take care also to provide fixed points where familiar words are repeated daily and get into our bones.

The three concepts of simplicity, continuity and variety all need to coincide in a Daily Office worthy of the name. We have achieved this as follows.

Simplicity
The simplicity of a clear structure which remains the same in each season's version of *Daily Prayer* and which is echoed in the shorter forms.

Continuity
Continuity through the course of each season with daily use of that season's Opening, Invitatory, Opening Prayer, Canticle of the Season, Intercessory Responses, and Conclusion, as well as daily use of the Lord's Prayer and a handful of other texts which never vary.

Variety
Sevenfold variety through the days of the week in each season with each day's Canticle and Responsory; a different set of seven in each season. Variety with the sets of four Concluding Prayers in each season, and of course through the recitation of the psalms appointed, and the reading of the Scriptures.

SACRED POETRY

The poetic prayers and praises of the Jewish people, the psalms, were the prayers and praises of Jesus and of Christians from the earliest days. Praying the psalms has been the Church's way of participating in the prayer of Christ over the ages. Yet plenty of other texts, scriptural and otherwise, fulfil a similar function. The Canticles stand alongside the psalms to provide the psalmody element of *Daily Prayer*.

THE PSALMS

Daily Prayer follows the Benedictine and Anglican traditions of making use of the entire Psalter, including those psalms which do not convert easily into Christian prayer. However, some psalms occur in our tables more often than others. So, for example, psalms 67, 84, 146 and 147 are used seven times each year, while psalms 20, 39, 59 and 140 are used only once. Prominence for some psalms and less frequent use of others allows a balance of psalmody more in tune with the hope of the gospel. The psalms are also distributed seasonally so that in *Joyful Hope* they strike a note of anticipation; in *Word Made Flesh*, revelation; in *Penitence*, discipleship; and in *New Life*, celebration. Of course some psalms occur in more than one season, and more general ones are distributed during the period *Through the Year*.

A number of psalms or psalm portions occur frequently elsewhere: the invitatories in *Daily Prayer* and those used in the shorter forms. Such use is in addition to their occurrence in the Lectionary.

Some Psalters place the more violent parts of psalmody in parentheses and it is up to the user whether or not to say these verses, but we have deliberately avoided being prescriptive in this matter.

THE CANTICLES

Until recently only a small number of texts other than the psalms were in regular use as the sacred poetry of the Church's daily prayer. Prominent among them were the three Gospel Canticles: the Song of Zechariah, the Song of Mary, and the Song of Simeon. *Daily Prayer*, in common with all recent versions of Daily Office, presents many more texts as Canticles, including some that we believe to be completely new.

It is worth considering the possibility of singing at least the Canticle of the Season, if not the other canticles and psalms. A number of simple chanting methods, such as that of Dom Gregory Murray, are easy to adapt to any words.

HYMNS AND ACCLAMATIONS

Use of a hymn is an opportunity to extend the use of sacred poetry in daily prayer to include so much more of the riches of the Christian tradition, ancient and recent. Most hymns can be said just as well as sung, which is, after all, how we have been treating the psalms for a very long time.

SCRIPTURE READING

In compiling the Lectionary for *Daily Prayer* we have tried to bear in mind that the Bible reading is being done as part of a period of prayer and worship. We have therefore not attempted to include the whole Bible, but those parts of it that we feel may be helpful devotionally. Thus while only 292 chapters of the 779 in the Old Testament are used, 238 chapters of the 260 in the New Testament are. During the seasons there is a single scheme of reading that is repeated every year, while in *Through the Year* there is a three-year cycle, which reflects the years in use in the Revised Common Lectionary.

One reading is provided for each day to enable you to focus on a single book of the Bible. The readings vary in length, as wherever possible we have tried to use natural breaks in a narrative. We have set longer passages when they form a complete story, while splitting closely argued theology into rather shorter sections. Where a reading uses edited portions of a chapter you are of course free to read the whole passage and fill in any other gaps in the reading of Bible books.

The Season of Joyful Hope begins with an edited reading from the prophecies of Isaiah. This is followed by the letters of St Paul to the Thessalonians with their strong themes of the coming end time. Around the beginning of Advent there are individual Gospel readings concerning John the Baptist and some of our Lord's sayings about the end, and then the season concludes with a more or less complete reading of the first part of the Book of Daniel.

The Season of the Word Made Flesh begins with a complete reading of the first letter of St John. Individual passages are chosen for Christmas Eve and Day and the saints' days following. This is followed by an edited reading of the Letter to the Hebrews. After the Epiphany we read a number of accounts of God's self-revelation to individuals from the Old Testament, culminating in his revelation to us in his Son as described in the first chapter of Hebrews. Then we read the letter of St Paul to the Ephesians. The season is concluded with the beginning of the Gospel of St John, which will be continued in Lent after a period of *Through the Year* that may be as little as a few days, or longer than a month, depending on the date of Easter.

During the seasons of *Penitence*, *Passion*, *Resurrection*, and *New Life* it is impossible to continue with a Lectionary based on the calendar date as these seasons move with the date of Easter. It is therefore necessary to know which week of Lent or Eastertide we are in, though of course the seasons do follow chronologically, so once you have begun on Ash Wednesday there is only a problem if for some reason you do not use *Daily Prayer* for a few days. In *The Season of New Life* the numbering of the Weeks of Eastertide corresponds with that of the Revised Common Lectionary, rather than those in the *Book of Common Prayer*.

In *The Season of Penitence* we read most of St John's Gospel, interrupted on Sundays with passages from Jeremiah.

In *The Season of the Passion*, the readings are mostly individually chosen to fit the days of Holy Week, and St John's Gospel is continued with the reading of chapter 17 on Maundy Thursday (we have deliberately left out the Passion narrative from chapters 18 and 19 as these are always read during the Good Friday Liturgy).

In *The Season of the Resurrection*, during Easter Week, we read the story of the Exodus.

The Season of New Life begins in the second week of Eastertide and first of all we complete the reading of St John's Gospel with the resurrection accounts. This is followed by St Paul's exposition of the resurrection from 1 Corinthians 15 and a complete reading of the first letter of St Peter. There is then an edited reading of Revelation, while the readings in the sixth and seventh weeks are chosen individually, firstly to lead up to the Ascension, and then to focus our minds on the coming of the Holy Spirit at Pentecost.

The Lectionary for *Through the Year* enables us to use the remaining parts of Scripture that were not included in these principal seasons, distributed over a three-year cycle.

Through the Year is used from 3 February to Shrove Tuesday inclusive, and then from the Monday following Pentecost until 31 October. The whole of this period is once more based on the calendar date. Where possible we have used the occurrence of saints' days as natural breaks in the Lectionary, and a suitable time to change to a different book of the Bible, though inevitably there are times when a saint's day does interrupt the reading of a book.

Until such time as the Churches might agree to fix the date of Easter there is always going to be a problem in how to work out a scheme of reading that takes its moveability into account. Our solution to this problem is that the readings set between the earliest and latest date that Lent can begin, are repeated between the earliest and latest date that Eastertide can end, so that wherever you break off in the scheme of readings at the beginning of Lent, you will resume there after Pentecost. Inevitably there will be some discontinuity in this reading but there is no way that this could be avoided. Because of the occurrence of a couple of saints' days in the immediate post-Pentecost period it is possible that one passage may be missed or repeated in years when Easter is particularly early or late. The problem of 29 February, which although only occurring in leap years can be in any of the three liturgical years, was solved by allocating the letter of St Jude to this date whenever it occurs. However, you will find that you do not in fact read this letter every four years as it will be read only in those years where 29 February occurs but does not fall during Lent. In practice you will find that Jude is read about as often as it ought to be!

The great story of the Old Testament as recorded from Genesis to Nehemiah is divided into six 'sagas', read in two sections in each of the three years. The Acts of the Apostles similarly splits conveniently into three sections so a portion of this is read each year.

Apart from the remaining three days after the feast of Saints Simon and Jude (29–31 October) where we read from the minor prophets, *Through the Year* ends with a more or less complete reading of the synoptic Gospel that has been read on Sundays that year in the Revised Common Lectionary.

Between 7 and 14 August in Years B and C we set passages from two Deutero-Canonical/Apocryphal books, Tobit and Maccabees, which we feel are worth reading. Should you not have these books in your Bible you will notice that in Year A they are paralleled by a reading of the letter of St Paul to the Philippians, and this can be read in all three years if preferred.

In Year B, on the four days leading up to the feast of St Peter and St Paul (29 June), which in some churches is the principal time for ordinations, there are readings on the theme of vocation and ministry. Should this theme be particularly relevant to you, or in your church, they may be used in one of the other years in place of the readings set.

Readings and psalms for saints' days are included in the scheme (except in the moveable seasons of *Penitence*, *Passion*, *Resurrection*, and *New Life*), with the suggestion that you use the order for *Saints' and Holy Days* for these celebrations, but even if you do not you will at least get something of the celebration of the saint within the context of the current season. Some of the readings chosen for saints' days have given us the opportunity to use individual passages that are not otherwise read during the course of the year.

In *Prayer Through the Day* very short Scripture passages are chosen, suitable to the seasons; while in the *Vigil of the Resurrection* the reading is always a Gospel of the Resurrection, except in Lent where it tends to be a Gospel foretelling Christ's passion.

The Lectionary is designed to complement the Revised Common Lectionary for Sundays and Festivals, and the Daily Eucharistic Lectionary used by the Roman Catholic Church and the Church of England and some other Churches. Thus only very rarely will the reading at *Daily Prayer* repeat one of the readings at a principal service in church, and on Saints' and Holy Days and throughout Lent and Easter it will complement those readings.

CONCLUSION

George Guiver CR wrote in 1988, 'There is a distinct possibility today that the daily office needs to pass through one of those transformations which have occasionally swept over it' (G. Guiver, *Company of Voices*, SPCK, 1988/Canterbury Press, 2001). His words were prophetic, as several recent initiatives and publications confirm. In compiling *Daily Prayer* we have sought to be faithful to the rich tradition of Christian corporate prayer, yet at the same time open to all the possibilities of 'transformation' in response to the contemporary circumstances and needs of Christian people.

Regular use of *Daily Prayer* – by lay people, as well as clergy; by busy people, as well as those with leisure time; in groups, as well as by individuals; in living rooms, offices and trains, as well as in churches; at coffee break, midday or rush hour, as well as morning and evening – will be the measure of our success.

COPYRIGHT
AND ACKNOWLEDGEMENTS

Strenuous efforts have been made to trace and request permission for all copyright material used in *Daily Prayer*. We apologise if we have inadvertently failed to acknowledge any such material and would undertake to correct this in any future edition.

We are grateful for permission to reproduce the following copyright material. Where one copyright holder has given permission for several texts to be used these are acknowledged individually and indexed by means of a superscript to the full copyright details which are given at the end of this section.

Loose card and inside front cover

The Lord's Prayer (modern version) is that prepared by the English Language Liturgical Commission (ELLC).[1]

The doxology 'Give praise to the Father . . .' which is also used after the Invitatories and Canticles of the Season and in the Opening of *Prayer Through the Day* and *Vigil of the Resurrection* is © The Grail, England.[7]

Openings

The seasonal Openings of *Daily Prayer* are drawn from the *Book of Alternative Services of the Anglican Church in Canada*.[2] *The Vigil of the Resurrection* (second Opening) is from St Augustine. Other Openings are adapted from Scripture by the compilers.[9]

Hymns and Acclamations

Bless the Lord, my soul; Gloria, gloria in excelsis Deo! (Gloria III); In the Lord I'll be ever thankful; Jesus, remember me; Nothing can trouble (Nada te Turbe); The Lord is my light; The Lord is my song; Wait for the Lord, whose day is near; are copyright © Ateliers et Presses de Taizé, 71250 Taizé-Community, France.

Do not be afraid, by Gerard Markland is copyright © Kevin Mayhew Ltd. Used by permission from *Complete Anglican Hymns Old & New*, Licence No. 107091.

Alleluia, alleluia, give thanks to the risen Lord (Alleluia No. 1), by Donald Fishel, is copyright © 1973 Word of God Music; Father, we adore you, by Terrye Coelho, is copyright © 1972 Maranatha! Music. Administered by CopyCare, PO Box 77, Hailsham BN27 3EF. music@copycare.com. Used by permission.

Abba, Father, let me be, by Dave Bilbrough is copyright © 1977 Kingsway's Thankyou Music; Jesus, Name above all names, by Nadia Hearn is copyright © 1974 Scripture in Song, a division of Integrity Music / Adm. by Kingsway's Thankyou Music, PO Box 75, Eastbourne, East Sussex BN23 6NW, UK. Used by kind permission of Kingsway's Thankyou Music.

Calm me, Lord, as you calmed the storm, by David Adam is © SPCK.[6]

Opening Prayers

The Opening Prayers are original compositions by the compilers.[9]

Psalms

The psalms in *Prayer Through the Day*; *Vigil of the Resurrection*; and the Invitatories in *Daily Prayer* are © The Grail, England.[7]

Scripture Readings

The short Scripture Readings in *Prayer Through the Day* are from the New Revised Standard Version of the Bible, Anglicised edition.[8]

Responsories

The responsories are adapted, mostly from Scripture, by the compilers.[9]

Canticles

The/A Song of: Mary; Zechariah; Simeon; the Church, are prepared by the English Language Liturgical Commission (ELLC).[1]

A Song of the Blessed and A Song of the Servant are from the *Book of Alternative Services of the Anglican Church in Canada*.[2]

The Easter Song of Praise is from *Lent, Holy Week, Easter* © The Archbishops' Council.[4]

The/A Song of: Christ the Servant; Christ's Appearing; Creation (adapted); Deliverance; Faith; Faith and Hope; God's Assembled; God's Grace; God's Reign; God's Love; Humility; Lamentation; Moses and of the Lamb; New Life; Peace; Praise; Redemption; Solomon; the Bride; the Lamb; the Messiah; the New Creation; the New Jerusalem; the Redeemed; the Redeemer; the Righteous; the Wilderness; Christ's Glory; Moses and Miriam; True Motherhood; and The Easter Anthems are used with permission from *Celebrating Common Prayer*, which is © The European Province of the Society of St Francis 1992.

The Slavonic Hymn of the Resurrection is © 1983 Dominican Nuns, Monastery of Our Lady, Summit, New Jersey, and is used with permission.

A Song of Christ's Goodness is compiled by and © The Revd Michael Vasey, and used with permission.

A Song of God's Gladness; A Song of Grace and Renewal are drawn from the New Revised Standard Version of the Bible, Anglicised edition.[8]

The/A Song of: the Lord's Return; the Gospel of God; God's Generosity; the Word of the Lord; Desertion are adapted from Scripture by the compilers [9]

Introductions to The Lord's Prayer

Original compositions by the compilers.[9]

Prayer and Thanksgiving Responses

The Season of Joyful Hope – adapted from *Patterns for Worship* © The Archbishops' Council.[4]

The Season of Penitence – from the Te Deum, prepared by the English Language Liturgical Commission (ELLC).[1]

The Season of New Life – adapted with permission from *Lent, Holy Week, Easter* © The Archbishops' Council.[4]

Through the Year – from *A New Zealand Prayer Book* – *He Karakia Mihinare o Aotearoa*.[3]

Saints and Holy Days – from *Patterns for Worship* (author unknown, from John 17) © The Archbishops' Council.[4]

The Season of the Word Made Flesh (from Scripture); and *The Seasons of the Passion and Resurrection* – compilers.[9]

Concluding Prayers

The Season of Joyful Hope

1. © The Revd Peter Grant Gardner, with permission.
2. St Gregory Nazianzen.
3. David Adam, adapted with permission from *Tides and Seasons* © SPCK.[6]
4. The Serenity Prayer by Reinhold Niebuhr is © and used by permission of Christopher Niebuhr. It has been adapted, with permission, by the addition of the words in italics in the text.

The Season of the Word Made Flesh

1. © The Revd Peter Grant Gardner, with permission.
2. St Augustine.
3. David Adam, from *Tides and Seasons* © SPCK.[6]
4. © Richard J. Foster, 'A Prayer of Covenant', from *Prayers from the Heart* (Hodder & Stoughton, London, 1995, p. 33), with permission.

The Season of Penitence

1. From the *Book of Alternative Services of the Anglican Church in Canada*.[2]
2. St Richard of Chichester.
3. *Carmina Gaedelica*.
4. Betty Hares.

The Season of the Passion

1. Janet Morley, from *All Desires Known* © SPCK.[6]

The Season of the Resurrection

1. From *A New Zealand Prayer Book* – *He Karakia Mihinare o Aotearoa*.[3]

The Season of New Life

1. From *A New Zealand Prayer Book* – *He Karakia Mihinare o Aotearoa*.[3]
2. Synesius of Cyrene.
3. Author unknown.
4. © Kathy Galloway, Glasgow, with permission.

Through the Year

1. From *A New Zealand Prayer Book* – *He Karakia Mihinare o Aotearoa*.[3]
2. St Augustine.
3. St Columba.
4. © The Very Revd Peter Baelz, for the Diocese of Durham, with permission.

Saints and Holy Days
1. From the *Book of Alternative Services of the Anglican Church in Canada*.[2]
2. Attributed to St Francis of Assisi.
3. The Venerable Bede.
4. Compilers[9] (from Ephesians 3:17–19).

Vigil of the Resurrection
1. Compilers.[9]
2. St Columba.
3. David Adam, adapted with permission from *Tides and Seasons* © SPCK.[6]
4. Author unknown.

Prayer in the Morning
1. From Morning Prayer, *The Alternative Service Book 1980* © The Archbishops' Council.[4]
2. Erasmus.
3. From *Carmina Gaedelica*, paraphrased by Alison Newell in *A Wee Worship Book* © WGRG, Iona Community.[5]
4. Christina Rosetti.

Prayer in the Evening
1. Traditional.
2. St Augustine.
3. From *A Wee Worship Book* © WGRG, Iona Community.[5]
4. © The Rt Revd Peter Nott, with permission.

Conclusions

The Season of Joyful Hope is from the New Revised Standard Version of the Bible, Anglicised edition.[8]

The Season of The Word Made Flesh – compilers.[9]

The Seasons of Penitence; *Passion*; and *Saints and Holy Days* are adapted from Seasonal Blessings in *Common Worship* (Holy Communion Order One) © The Archbishops' Council.[4]

The Season of New Life is adapted with permission from *A New Zealand Prayer Book – He Karakia Mihinare o Aotearoa*.[3]

The Seasons of the Passion and the Resurrection (Easter Week), and the *Vigil of the Resurrection* are from Hippolytus.

Through the Year is from St Paul.

Prayer in the Morning is from the *Book of Alternative Services of the Anglican Church in Canada*.[2]

Prayer in the Evening is traditional.

Index to copyright holders referenced in the above list by superscript